B. D. Amis,
African American Radical

A Short Anthology of Writings and Speeches

Edited by

Walter T. Howard

University Press of America,® Inc.

Lanham · Boulder · New York · Toronto · Plymouth, UK

Copyright © 2007 by
University Press of America,® Inc.
4501 Forbes Boulevard
Suite 200
Lanham, Maryland 20706
UPA Acquisitions Department (301) 459-3366

Estover Road
Plymouth PL6 7PY
United Kingdom

Library of Congress Control Number: 2006930460
ISBN-13: 978-0-7618-3581-3 (paperback : alk. paper)
ISBN-10: 0-7618-3581-4 (paperback : alk. paper)

Dedicated to
Stephanie, Chris, Ian, Austin, and Virginia
and
Lowell Howard, Sr.
and
Walter Howard

CONTENTS

PREFACE

Virtually unknown today, and often overlooked by historians, African American Communist B.D. Amis was a major figure in the black freedom struggle during the two decades between the world wars. At that time, the American Communist Party (CPUSA) played a significant role in fighting for the rights of African Americans. In those years, Amis was part of the small circle of black radicals leading the struggle for workers' rights and racial justice. This short anthology of his key writings and speeches reveals the deep commitment to the working class of his generation of African American Marxists.

After a comprehensive introduction by Amis's son, Barry D. Amis, this anthology begins with "Lynch Justice at Work." A 1930 CPUSA pamphlet penned by Amis, it offers a cogent Marxist analysis of lynchings and the southern racial caste system. Chapter 2 presents nine key press articles written by Amis and published in the *Daily Worker* in 1930-31. They dealt with Communist recruitment of African Americans, the American Negro Labor Congress, the League of Struggle for Negro Rights, the Marion (Indiana) lynching, criticism of Marcus Garvey, the solidarity between white and black workers, and especially attacks on white chauvinism inside of the American Communist movement. The CPUSA respected Amis in terms of his theoretical contributions, and published two of his analytic essays in the Party's theoretical organ, *The Communist*. Chapter 4 deals with Amis's efforts on behalf of the Scottsboro youths, including his memorable article, "They Shall Not Die," which appeared in *The Liberator* (LSNR publication) in 1931. The next chapter presents Amis's speech to the 1936 national CPUSA convention in Chicago that nominated William Z. Foster for president, as well as two other radio speeches that Amis delivered in his 1936 campaign for Auditor-General in Pennsylvania. Chapter 6 offers some of Amis's work in 1933 when he was district organizer in the industrial center of Cleveland, Ohio. In 1934-35 he traveled to the Soviet Union for training as a Party leader. At this time he wrote several pieces for the *International Press Correspondence* that attacked the First New Deal and the National Recovery Administration, and also criticized former Communist George Padmore. Chapter 8 presents writings by Amis in the late 1930s when he was a very active and highly successful CIO and SWOC operative in Philadelphia. The Epilogue offers one Amis letter in the forties followed by a brief summary of his life after being victimized by McCarthyism in the late forties and fifties.

The book also has important international documents as well as a selected bibliography of scholarship on African Americans and Communism.

Walter T. Howard
Bloomsburg, PA
January 12, 2006

ACKNOWLEDGMENTS

This book could not have been edited without the assistance of many people. I declare my debt to all of them. First and foremost I need to thank the children of B.D. Amis, especially Debbie Amis Bell and Barry D. Amis. Both were generous with their time and information about their father. They also freely shared all the papers and documents of their father.

Both have been successful African Americans in their respective fields of endeavor. Debbie A. Bell has made significant contributions to the Civil Rights Movement, the Labor Movement, and the movement fighting for quality public education. Her credentials as an authentic and committed American radical are impressive. She is the current Chairperson of the Communist Party of Eastern Pennsylvania and Delaware, a founding member and Treasurer of the Black Radical Congress, a former Executive Board Member of the Philadelphia Federation of Teachers, a former member of the AFL-CIO Central Labor Council, a founding member and former Treasurer of the Labor Party, former Field Secretary for the Student Non-violent Coordinating Committee, and a retired Philadelphia public school teacher.

Barry D. Amis became an important African American figure in the field of education. He has taught as a professor at Michigan State University and Purdue University; he was also a Fulbright Professor in France, Cameroon, and Niger. He was a pioneer in the development of African American literature courses at Michigan State. Dr. Amis is Regional Director for the Association for Supervision and Curriculum Development in Virginia. Finally, he is the former Director, Staff Development Initiatives, in Montgomery County, Maryland public schools.

Three historians of American Communism, Edward Johanningsmeier, John Earl Haynes, and Vernon Pedersen, were helpful as I utilized material from the files of the Communist Party of the United States (CPUSA) at the Library of Congress in Washington, D.C.. I also want to thank all the helpful archivists and librarians at Penn State University's Historical Collection and Labor Archives and at New York University's Tamiment Institute Archive. Ann Diseroad, current director of the Interlibrary Loan Department at Bloomsburg University, rendered me invaluable services in locating and obtaining important historical material for this study.

Many thanks to my academic home, the history department at Bloomsburg University. I want again to acknowledge my department chairperson, William V. Hudon, for his help and encouragement in this and all research projects. Thanks also go to the stalwart Joyce Bielen for her help in this and all other similar endeavors in publishing important research.

INTRODUCTION
B.D. AMIS—BLACK COMMUNIST
AND LABOR LEADER

[*People's Weekly World*, November 20, 2004
by Barry D. Amis]

While little known today, during the late 1920s and the 1930s, B.D. Amis was one of a small cadre of African Americans leading the fight for workers' rights and racial justice. Urbane in demeanor and a dynamic speaker, he was one of the most important Black activists of his time. His commitment was to the working class and, in particular, the Black working class.

Amis was born in Chicago in 1896. In his youth he was influenced by the anti-lynching writings of pioneering journalist and civil rights crusader Ida B. Wells-Barnett, who became his mentor while he was still in high school.

Amis became politically active in the early 1920s and by 1928 was president of the NAACP branch in Peoria, Ill. He addressed many civic and church groups about the activities and goals of the NAACP and gave speeches in defense of the rights of his people. A May 1928 article in *The Peoria Journal* described him as a man who "has a pleasing personality and made a deep impression upon his hearers this morning."

After discussions at the 1928 congress of the Communist International, the Communist Party USA had pledged to take up the "Negro Question." The CPUSA leadership invited Amis to come to New York after seeing his effectiveness as a local activist. The party's determination to address the issue of Black rights was extraordinary because almost no other non-Black organization was willing to address this issue in the 1920s and 1930s.

Amis was also one of the first native born and working-class Black leaders of the party. Other early Black Communist leaders, such as Cyril Briggs and Otto Huiswoud, had been born in the Caribbean and had college educations.

Communism's appeal to Blacks

It is not surprising that the Communist platform was attractive to African Americans in the 1920s and the 1930s. The Black community still strongly felt the legacy of slavery and the betrayal of Reconstruction. There were also thousands of Black soldiers who had fought for democracy in World War I, only to return home to an America rife with Jim Crow laws, segregation, discrimination, lynching, and near-peonage for many southern Black farmers.

Black workers were generally excluded from labor unions. With the onset of the Great Depression in 1929, Black workers, who already were suffering economically, lost jobs by the tens of thousands. Three to four times as many Blacks as whites ended up on the relief rolls in urban areas. The Communist Party, by virtue of its openness to Blacks and willingness to take up the Negro Question, became the choice for Amis and other prominent Blacks of the era.

The NAACP and Marcus Garvey's Universal Negro Improvement Association, also known as the Back to Africa movement, were other organizations vying to represent the interests and needs of the Black population at that time.

W.E.B. Du Bois, the editor of the NAACP magazine *The Crisis*, had proposed his idea of educating the best and most capable Blacks, a "Talented Tenth." Garvey was interested in racial uplift through Black economic and political independence. The party, however, offered a political arena and an activist agenda to deal with the Negro Question that these organizations eschewed.

Writer, speaker, mass leader

As a member of the National Committee of the American Negro Labor Congress (ANLC), Amis plunged wholeheartedly into CPUSA activities and quickly became one of its most visible members. He recruited, organized rallies, spoke at conferences, and wrote articles for the *Daily Worker*, the CPUSA's newspaper and predecessor of the *People's Weekly World*.

Articles such as "ANLC as Mass Organization of Negro Workers," "Vote Communist—Negro Workers," "Fight Against White Chauvinism," "Negro Workers Are Hard Hit by Unemployment; Must Organize," and others are indicative of the issues that concerned not only him but also the party as a whole.

In 1930, Amis became the general secretary of the newly formed League of Struggle for Negro Rights (LSNR) and an editor of its publication, *The Liberator*. The role of the LSNR was to publicize the issues of the day, especially lynching, through rallies, conferences and picketing. The well-known Black poet Langston Hughes was the group's honorary president.

Among its other activities, in 1933 the LSNR drafted a "Bill of Rights for the Negro People," which was carried to Washington by 3,500 demonstrators demanding that the Franklin D. Roosevelt administration enforce the Constitution and give Black Americans their rights.

Aside from his engagement with many movements for social justice and equality, Amis was involved in three of the most celebrated political frame-up cases of his time: the Scottsboro case, the Angelo Herndon case, and the case of Tom Mooney.

The Scottsboro 9

In 1931, just after he had written the pamphlet "Lynch Justice at Work," came the event that was to epitomize lynch justice and symbolize the oppression of Black Americans: the Scottsboro case. Nine Black youths riding on a freight train were falsely accused of raping two white women.

Today it is hard to imagine the resonance that the case had in the 1930s. It pitted Southern lynch justice against the legal challenge to racism and discrimination, the more conservative NAACP leadership against the more militant Communist Party, and the power of direct action against the passiveness of the legal process.

The party immediately recognized the significance of what was happening and acted swiftly to organize the defense for the nine accused youths through the International Labor Defense (ILD). Amis contributed to the defense effort as author of the pamphlet "They shall not die! The story of Scottsboro in pictures," put out by the LSNR. The cry, "They shall not die!" spread not only throughout the United States, but across Europe as well.

The strategic decision to organize mass demonstrations, to issue posters, and to write articles brought national and international publicity that ultimately saved the lives of the accused.

Amis was deeply involved in all of this, including traveling to Alabama. The virulent racism spurred a clamoring for the deaths of the accused in spite of the overwhelming proof of their innocence. The party took an open and committed stand against racism and injustice, thereby enhancing its standing in the Black community.

The success of the activist tactics of the Scottsboro case would eventually lead to A. Philip Randolph's proposed March on Washington in 1941, the Montgomery bus boycott, the 1963 March on Washington, and the civil rights movement. The LSNR and the ILD demonstrated that picket lines, pamphlets, posters, magazine and newspaper articles and anti-lynching rallies could be effective tactics in the fight for workers' rights and justice for African Americans.

Herndon and Mooney

The very next year, 1932, 20-year-old Angelo Herndon, a member of the Young Communist League, was arrested in Atlanta and later sentenced to 18-20 years on a Georgia chain gang for attempting to "incite insurrection" based on his possession of Communist literature. Soon the ILD was leading a nationwide campaign for his freedom.

Herndon wrote in his autobiography, "Let Me Live," that at the first All-Southern Conference for the Scottsboro Defense in Chattanooga, May 31, 1931, "Perhaps the most eloquent address of the meeting was made by B.D. Amis. . . . He brought both whites and Negroes to their feet cheering loudly. So great was the enthusiasm and militancy of the audience that the cops looked scared."

The third highly visible case that Amis had a connection to was that of the militant labor leader Tom Mooney, who had been convicted of a bombing in San Francisco. Mooney was sentenced to death, later reduced to life, even though the evidence against him was shown to have been faked and several witnesses' testimony was proven false. Amis read a statement written by Tom Mooney's aged mother Mary to a crowd of 12,000 at the Bronx Coliseum in February 1932.

Further recognition of the stature that Amis had during this period is Nancy Cunard's inclusion of his essay, "The Negro National Oppression and Social Antagonisms," in her seminal anthology, "Negro." The list of contributors to this now classic work looks like a Who's Who of the 1920s and 1930s. Amis was right there among them.

Party and union leader

Amis went on to become the district organizer for the Communist Party in Cleveland for a couple of years and traveled to the Soviet Union on two occasions. The second trip lasted about a year-and-a-half. While there, he took courses in Marxism, traveled with other Americans, such as Paul Robeson, and wrote articles for the *Negro Worker*, the newspaper of the International Trade Union Committee of Negro Workers.

Upon his return to the United States, Amis settled in Philadelphia and joined the Steel Workers Organizing Committee (SWOC) as a field organizer. He also was the head of the Philadelphia committee of the National Negro Congress, an organization established in 1936 to "secure the right of the Negro people to be free from Jim Crowism, segregation, discrimination, lynching, and mob violence" and "to promote the spirit of unity and cooperation between Negro and white people."

Amis was also the chairman of the Philadelphia Committee for the Defense of Ethiopia and member of another committee to raise funds for the defense of the Republican (anti-fascist) government of Spain. As if these activities were not enough, Amis also ran as the Communist candidate for auditor general of Pennsylvania in 1936 and made an "Appeal to the Colored Voters to Vote Communist" on a local radio station.

By the late 1930s Amis had begun to shift from political activism to union organizing. He was having success with the SWOC and in two years had organized 15 groups of steelworkers into unions or lodges, negotiated union contracts, had acted as spokesman in labor board cases.

Among the companies organized were Lukens Steel, Allenwood Steel and the Pacific Steel Boiler Company. An article in the October 16, 1938, *Philadelphia Independent* said, "The labor press hailed his victory in organizing the J.E. Lovergan Company of Philadelphia, pointing out that for 100 years this had been a nonunion concern."

His success with the steel workers led the local joint board of the Hotel, Restaurant and Service Employees International Alliance and the Bartenders International League to ask him to organize the Black service workers in Philadelphia, who were subject to "unequaled exploitation," in the words of a trade unionist of that time.

Once again it didn't take long for Amis to have success. He organized Local 758 of the Colored Catering Industry Workers, and soon local newspapers were reporting that for its members in Philadelphia, "Wage increases have become effective for all cooks and kitchen employees, porters, etc., at leading caterers." He also won jobs for them at the new Cotton Club restaurant.

Unfortunately, Amis' success with Black workers brought resentment from white unions, who called upon the international union, headquartered in Detroit, to dismiss Amis and to have Local 758's business transacted through the local white union. This move demonstrated how embedded racism was in the AFL. This changeover in power eventually nullified many of the gains that Amis had won.

A unique vision

Amis' career represents a remarkable record of unrecognized achievement during an incredibly racist and anti-union period. The Communist Party made much of this possible through entities that led the fight for racial justice and workers' rights such as its Negro commission, the American Negro Labor Congress, the International Labor Defense, the Trade Union Unity League, the League of Struggle for Negro Rights and the National Negro Congress.

Perhaps if more people knew the stories of how ordinary individuals such as Amis (or Ned Cobb or Fannie Lou Hamer) rose to extraordinary achievement, they would be encouraged to take on the questionable activities of many of today's governmental and corporate leaders.

CHAPTER 1
LYNCH JUSTICE AT WORK
[CPUSA Pamphlet, New York, 1930]

During the first nine months of this year twenty-five Negroes have been lynched. This number more that doubles the number of lynchings of the entire year of 1929. The lynching of Negroes and mob terrorism have become the most effective weapon used by the "boss" class to keep the black and white workers divided and to lower the living standards of the entire working class. Lynchings rise in number and savage cruelty as the present economic crisis deepens. The white ruling class attempts to perpetuate hatred among the Negro and white workers through a carefully planned system of poisonous propaganda. Through lynchings this same class attempts to keep the workers more sharply divided and thereby prevent militant action on the part of the Negro masses to fight against their terrible exploitation and the most savage and brutal forms of oppression. As long as the black and white workers are divided, so long will the bosses be able to exploit the entire working class and wring still greater profits from their labor.

The Negro toilers feel the "impartiality" of the capitalist judicial machine which refuses to convict the terrorist agents of the bosses on charges of lynchings. A few accounts of the latter are given which show the utter necessity of conducting a decisive struggle against such atrocities.

A mob of 1,000 persons composed mainly of business men and respectable officials, took Jimmy Irvine, a Negro worker, from the custody of the sheriff at Ocilla, Georgia, and lynched him. To justify this barbarous act and make it appear as a "virtuous" act, the bosses press accusation was that Irvine had attacked the daughter of a farmer. A standard slanderous lie, that the bosses criminal agents always use to clear the lynchers.

A blood thirsty mob, led by the respectable local bankers and bosses, satisfied its lust by lynching a 65 year old Negro woman at Barbar's Junction, North Carolina. They had overlooked accusing this old grandmother of attempting to "rape" some virtuous white master's daughter. Such an excuse would hold good under this bosses lynch-justice of South.

In April, John H. Wilkins, a Pullman porter was taken from a train at Locust Grove, Ga., and lynched for no other reason that he smiled at a white woman in the performance of his duties. Only the "flowers" of southern knighthood, so noble and so upright, who have never raped a Negro young girl, can gaze upon such virtue, as a female white skin.

Dave Harris was shot to death by a mob of 250 men at Rosedale, Miss. This mob of degenerate agents of the landlords was filled with "race" hatred, the kind spread by the bosses to keep the workers divided. They did not realize that they were taking the life of a brother worker who belonged to the working class of which they were a part and which they were betraying by their acts.

Negro workers are not alone lynched, but white workers also. The bosses will have the Italian worker believe he is "better" than the Polish worker; the German worker "superior" to the Mexican worker, etc. Thereby, one group is pitted against another, and the bosses carry on their exploitive methods. Under such circumstances, John Hodaz, a white worker was lynched at Plant City, Fla.

In Walhalla, S.C., Allen Green, a 50 year old Negro worker, accused of attacking a white woman, was taken from jail and lynched by a mob which overpowered and injured the sheriff. As a result of an investigation, by the governor, four men were held and fifteen were released on bonds. After one postponement that seventeen lynchers were brought to trial. The judge declared that it was too hot to sit through long legal battles and discontinued the trial. Justice works in miraculous way when the workers and especially the Negro workers are involved. It is an unwritten law of the bosses that lynchers shall not be punished; it would be a travesty on their justice.

In Kansas, an insane Negro, Clarence Hayes, who escaped from the hospital was attacked by the sheriff and city marshal. In the fight that followed, the sheriff was killed, so it was said, by Hayes. How an unarmed insane man who was attacked by two armed city officials, could kill the sheriff we leave to be explained by the white exploiters of Kansas. A posse formed and pursued Hayes to a field. There he took refuge behind a grazing cow, but realizing his condition, he stepped out, hands in air, and offered to surrender. He was riddled with bullets.

One of the most barbarous crimes committed was by a mob of thousands of persons in Sherman, Texas. Leading and instigating this mob, were the business men of the town, the white ruling exploiters, the oppressors of the Negro toilers. They set fire to the Grayson County Court House, cremating alive George Hughes, a Negro worker. The charred body was taken from the ruins, fastened with a chain to a car and dragged through the streets of the Negro section. The lifeless body was strung to a tree. The business men then proceeded to destroy the property of the Negroes.

Within a week another Texas gang of the bosses' terrorists sent a Negro worker to a fiery sepulcher. The body of George Johnson was burned at

Honey Grove. Johnson had been ordered back to work by a farmer, but refused to go. The farmer seized a gun and attempted to force Johnson to work. Johnson momentarily forgot that he was in slavery and thought that he was a free man and could work when he so desired. Also he forgot that he should **not** defend himself but must cower before his master. But as he should have done and as all Negro and white workers must learn to do against lynch mobs, Johnson defended himself.

Jack Robertson, a Negro worker, for seeking to collect his wages from his employer of Round Rock, Texas, was attacked by the latter. In self-defense Robertson shot his employer and his wife. Because he sought to obtain wages which were rightfully due him, a posse of 150 planters hunted down the worker and lynched him.

All lynchings do not take place in the South. Marion, Ind., became the exponent of lynch-justice with a double lynching of two young Negroes, Tom Shipp, 18, and Abe Smith, 19. These youths were in jail awaiting trial. A mob of onlookers numbering close to 10,000 persons watched the respectable bosses and their agents perform this gruesome orgy. Without any resistance from the "law enforcer" the sheriff, members of the mob entered the jail and seized their victims. The terrified youths were dragged to the lawn of the courthouse and hanged to a tree. The perpetrators of this crime could get no nearer to the portals of justice than the court house lawn. But "justice" looked out of the court house window and we are positive it gave its consent to the terrible crime.

The deputy of Edgecombe jail in Tarboro, N.C., freely admitted a mob of terrorists who dragged out Olive Moore and shot him to death. The deputy explained that the leaders gained admittance to the jail by pretending that they had brought a prisoner. This was another lie hatched to cover up the willingness of the city officials to carry out the dictates of the bosses in subduing the militant spirit of struggle and resistance that is rising among the Negro masses.

The two major political parties in power, make no attempt to smash lynchings, because this is the unwritten law of the land enforced by their interests as exploiters of Negroes. A feeble "effort" was directed to crush this extra-legal apparatus of the bosses by the Dyer anti-lynching bill. This bill was passed in the House of Representatives but when it came to the Senate, the southern senators bitterly opposed it using the pretext that it would curb the state autonomy of the southern states. Consequently the bill died without a struggle but with the usual agreement of both Northern and Southern senators.

The gruesome lynchings of Negroes and other forms of organized violence are based directly on the need of the white landowners and capitalist class to perpetuate their system of double exploitation and severe oppression of the Negro family and workers. The Negro masses especially of the South are absolutely helpless and defenseless, because they enjoy no social or political rights and especially the right to defend themselves. In order that the Negro masses may be kept in their terrified and defenseless positions, frequent lynchings and all forms of violence are practiced by organizations, agents of the white "boss" class

Terrorist Organizations

The Negro masses of the United States are subjected and oppressed in the same way as the colonial peoples and oppressed minorities under the bloody heel of imperialist exploiters. The Negro masses must realize that the only way that their misery and oppression can be overcome is by organized struggle against their white oppressors. The success of this struggle depends upon a close alliance with the white workers who are exploited by the same white bosses who oppress and super exploit the Negroes.

The white workers, especially the revolutionary white workers, must give full and complete support to the demands of the Negro masses for full economic and political equality and the right for self-determination and must form a genuine united front in the struggle against their common enemy, the white ruling class.

For over 200 years, the Negroes were held in actual slavery. With the development of industrial capitalism in the North a movement developed by the industrial capitalists to establish their control over the Washington government. In order that the development of the northern industries could proceed unhampered, it was evident that slavery had to be abolished. Simultaneously the slave owners of the South were determined that their system of slave labor should prevail in the United States. The Civil War decided by force of arms which of the exploiting class should rule the American Empire.

Slavery as an institution was abolished by the northern capitalists with the assistance of Negro soldiers when the southern plantation owners were defeated. After the cessation of hostilities, the Negroes, who during the war failed to take the land from the slave owners, were granted "bourgeois democratic rights," that is, rights to franchisement, holding of public office, education, free speech, and assemblage, etc., equal to the privileges of the white workers. The Negroes were given a paper guarantee of social and political equality. But this did not last long. Friendly relations were established between the northern and southern "bourgeoisie," or exploiters, on the conditions of continued super-exploitation of the Negro toilers, or from their sweat and blood. The paper guarantee of social and political rights "granted" the Negro masses was ignored.

Before the Civil War, unwritten legal measures, backed by the armed might of the slave owners, kept the Negroes in subjection, but since, illegal, violent, unwritten lynch-law and special terrorist organizations have been the methods used to the same purpose.

In the North and South there exists a complete system of organizations which assist the white ruling class to keep the Negro people in a helpless state of terror and subjection so that they may bleed, plunder and rob the Negro toiling masses unhampered by strikes, resistance, or even protests. Open forms of persecution take place. Many Negro toilers are brutally beaten, tarred and feathered, driven out of town and thus forced to abandon their pitiful possessions.

The Ku Klux Klan which originated in Atlanta, Georgia, almost immediately after the Civil War "emancipated" the Negroes, boasts that the U.S.A. is a white man's country (meaning the white bosses' country), and must remain as such. It is the "defender of white supremacy" (meaning white bosses' supremacy), and the "protector" of "white womanhood" (the standard slanderous excuse for lynching Negro workers). It has in its ranks the respectable bankers, landowners, capitalists and their politicians, who put into force the policies of the Klan. This organization has wrought havoc among the Negro workers by use of the fiery cross, an indication of warning that the selected victim must leave the particular area, and the most brutal methods of persecution, such as lynching, whipping, etc.

The American Fascisti Order of Black Shirts was formed "to inculcate and foster in the minds of its members and the public generally, white supremacy." It has a secret membership like the Klan and has started a campaign "jobs for the white man," a miserable subterfuge to divide the exploited white workers from their super-exploited Negro comrades. In the South where Negroes are employed in the industrial centers, the American Fascisti endeavors to "persuade" the employers to discharge the Negro worker and to give employment to the white worker. "Threat" of boycott is used to obtain this end, but in reality it is another method to divide the exploited workers on race differences. In Atlanta 600 Negro workers such as truck drivers, porters, bellhops, etc., have been replaced by white workers through "forced" pressure of the organization.

The White Band of the Caucasian Crusaders is similar to the Klan. The ousted leader of the Klan is the organizer. It is "essentially and fundamentally an ethnic or racial movement of the white man." It preaches that the only hope of the white man is for him to unite and organize himself for self-protection of his blood, his interest and his breed. It agitates against the association and inter-marriage of Negro and white workers and directs a malicious tirade against the Negro masses. This too is a vicious organization of the white bosses used to justify and protect the policy of plundering the Negroes.

The overcrowding of Negro-ghettos in northern metropolitan centers has caused many Negroes to invade white residential neighborhoods. Protective Home Owners Clubs have sprung up to bar Negroes from restricted districts.

In Chicago, the Lithuanian Business Men's Association conducts a bitter campaign to bar Negroes from purchasing or renting homes in Bridgeport. By use of violence and force, Negroes are kept out of this territory.

In Columbia Heights, Washington, D.C., the Columbia Heights Forum, through a pamphlet, called the white citizens to get together to oppose Negro neighbors just as impersonally as they would oppose floods, impassable streets, unsightly buildings or anything else that would cheapen the value of their homes. Always we find the economic motive behind the race superiority phrases.

These mobs and terrorist organizations are not hoodlums, or idiots, but are a part of the systematic apparatus of oppression. Such societies in a careful planned manner corrupt the working class with false and ruinous ideas which on the one hand, help to hide the real intentions of the white bosses, and on the other, prevent the building of a united front of Negro and white workers to pit their united strength against the white ruling exploiters.

The real cause of these extra legal measures, to keep the Negroes in subjection, is not because they are a "black race" or a group of people with curly hair and dark skin. It is because of the economic conditions of the Negro masses which enables the white ruling class to derive greater profits from them through a system of double exploitation. The Negroes are doubly exploited, first, because they belong to the working class; second, because they are economically an oppressed minority group. Special forms of persecution, lynching and mob terrorism, are for the purpose of keeping them in this situation.

The super exploitation of the Negro masses reduces them to the lowest possible living scale. Bitter oppression and hatred has forced the Negro toiler into rural and industrial black belts. In these territories they experience conditions that are unbelievable.

Economic Conditions

The living conditions of the Negro toilers are considerably lower than those of the average white workers. In the large industrial centers the unwritten law of Jim-Crowism crowds them into Negro-ghettos. For the worst shacks and hovels they pay the highest rents. Many Negro quarters have no sewers, the streets are bad and unlighted. So terrible are the housing conditions that the death-rate of Negroes is much higher than that of the white.

In the South Negro children are given a limited education in Jim-Crow schools, which exist in some parts of the North also. Four to five times more funds are appropriated for the Southern white child than for the Negro. The following table gives the average annual expenditure per child, school age:

State	White	Negro
Alabama	$26.57	$3.81
Florida	42.01	7.33
So. Carolina	27.88	2.74
Mississippi	25.95	5.62
Texas	31.77	20.24
Arkansas	13.36	6.48

The Negro teachers receive from one fourth to one third the salary of white teachers. The schools are generally old, dilapidated buildings and are open from four to six months in the year. In the North the situation is not much better. There are fewer Jim-Crow schools and Negro children are given better opportunities to obtain an education. However, segregation is practiced on a large scale. In the mess halls, dormitories, and on the athletic field, Negro students are generally barred. In the large cities, the Negro neighborhoods are poorly kept. Bad housing conditions, over crowded areas and unsanitary quarters prevail in every "black belt."

The Negro toilers, poor farmers and agricultural workers, are of the most highly exploited section of the working class. This double exploitation of the Negro masses dates back to slavery days, when the Negro was first brought to this country and used to slave in the cotton and tobacco fields of the South.

In the South the agricultural laborers, sharecroppers and tenant farmers live under semi-feudal oppression. These toilers are practically chained to the land owned by the white ruling class. About 80% of the millions of Negroes in the South live in the farming areas. Few of them own their own farms. In many instances the few who own their farms have them heavily mortgaged. Live stock and implements, likewise the crops are mortgaged to the white banker or plantation owner. Consequently the farmer is forced to sacrifice his crops and has the threat of eviction or jail constantly staring him in the face for failure to pay his exorbitant obligations. The farm laborer is virtually a slave, often held against his will and paid the lowest wages. The wages frequently are so low as $18.20 a month. From these wages come deductions for food, clothing and tools. Once in debt, the Negro farm laborer is forced to remain on the farm until the debt is worked out. This very seldom happens. Often times claims for debts are sold or transferred with the laborer. If he attempts to escape this barbarous exploitation, a system of vagrancy laws and debt imprisonment await him. Convict lease labor or the chain gang are the results. The penalty is not always applied in this method, but whippings, lynchings and shootings frequently are substituted for the chain gang.

In the South there exist "hidden" plantations where Negro men and women are held in virtual slavery. Slave trade exists in a concealed form. These toilers are forced to work without receiving any wages and with the assistance of armed guards, the farm bosses prevent them from ever leaving the colony without permission.

This vicious system of double exploitation and oppression has caused many of the poor farmers and agricultural laborers to migrate North. They exchange the persecution in the South for a highly intensified industrial exploitation in the North. In such industrial centers as Chicago, Pittsburgh and Detroit, there is a fast-growing Negro industrial proletariat. These workers are given the dirtiest most menial jobs and receive the lowest pay. They work from ten to sixteen hours a day for wages much lower than are paid to white workers who do the same kind of work.

During hard times they are the first to have their wages cut and receive lay-offs. Because they are unable to pay the extra high rents (especially during economic crises) they are evicted from their homes. This cheap, unorganized and docile labor has been a weapon used by the white ruling class to worsen the economic conditions of the entire working class.

Growth of Unemployment

The development of unemployment has taken a heavy toll among the Negro toilers. Thousands have been thrown upon the streets by the economic crisis and the cutting down of production.

During and after the last war, thousands of Negro workers were brought into the North by the white ruling bosses, to work in the industrial centers. Other thousands came, hoping to better their conditions and escape the barbarous southern persecution. The Negro workers, who took the place of the white workers, were thrown into the streets upon the termination of hostilities and return of the latter, jobless and abandoned to their fate. During the crisis immediately following the war, Negro unemployed workers suffered untold and bitter hardships. Most avenues of skilled and unskilled workers were closed to them.

The deep going economic crisis of today numbers among its growing millions of unemployed, hundreds of thousands of Negro workers. The white bosses who place the burden of the crisis on the entire working class, give the Negroes "full equality" to bear more than their share of the burden. The stock yards in Chicago first layed off thousands of Negro workers. The steel mills of Gary layed off Negro workers before the whites. From an estimated number of 400,000 unemployed in Chicago, 10% are Negro workers. A textile factory in the South discharged 400 Negro women and youth in one week. The average wage of theses workers was a little less than $5.00 per week. It was impossible for them to have saved any of their wages while working. Consequently to lose their jobs meant to face misery and starvation.

The areas recently laid waste by the drought numbered many Negro laborers and farmers. These toilers are facing starvation, because all relief that has been promised contains an "if" clause, i.e., if they (the farmers) have security, relief will be given by the government. The Negro tenant farmers have no security. In most cases what little they possess, is mortgaged.

Many of the poor farmers and agricultural laborers leave the farming areas for the industrial centers in vain search for work. The drought has caused many more to leave, who in all likelihood would have remained on their farms. Consequently their invasion of the industrial centers adds to the army of unemployed.

Solidarity of Negro and White Workers

The increased number of lynchings this year vividly shows that the white ruling class and its agents instigate and encourage lynchings as one of the methods to defeat the rising spirit of revolt and action among the Negro and white workers.

The Negro toilers cannot expect the three bosses' political parties (which constitute Gerard's 59 rules and their agents) to struggle in their behalf against lynchings and mob terrorism. The Republican Party has nothing to offer the Negro workers and peasants but terror, growing unemployment, deeper misery and wage cuts. The mass unemployment and mass lay-offs of the year have destroyed all illusions of the Republican Party as a party of "prosperity" and of the Negro toilers. It has no solution for lynch-laws and unemployment, because it is directly responsible for both. The entire burden of these two evils are placed on the Negro toilers and white workers.

The Democratic Party openly stands for the oppression and persecution of Negroes. One of the chief spokesman of the party has openly endorsed lynching. In a statement delivered at a mass meeting at Union, South Carolina, this spokesman, Senator Cole Blease said, "whenever the constitution of the United States comes between me and the virtue of white women of South Carolina, I say to hell with the constitution." Continuing his tirade, the Democratic senator declared, "white supremacy and the protection of the virtue of white women of the South comes first with me." "When I was governor of South Carolina you did not hear of me calling out the state militia to protect Negro rapists. In all my campaigns you heard me say 'when you catch the brute that assaults a white woman, wait until the next morning to notify me'." These words speak clearly. They incite, encourage and endorse mob terrorism and lynching. It was due to the initiative of the Democratic Party senators that all attempts to legislate against lynching were defeated, by a gentlemanly agreement of all senators.

The Socialist Party, third party of the bosses, acting as the betrayer and misleader of the working class, has joined with the terrorist organizations in a most malignant attack upon Negro workers. *The New Leader*, official organ of the Socialist Party, states very plainly the position of the Party to the Negro masses. In the state convention at Virginia the Socialist misleaders of labor declared the racial problem most difficult to solve. "Almost all southerners believe in segregating the Negro and depriving him of social and political rights that whites enjoy. The southern Socialists must adjust their tactics to this state of affairs. The northern leaflets, pamphlets, and newspapers are frequently useless, if not harmful in the South. It is certain that there will never be a thriving Socialist movement in the South unless it is conducted in southern style. The Socialists of Virginia are good Socialists as well as southerners and can be trusted to solve the intricate problems involved. They will be worthy of the best Socialist traditions."

In this manner the Socialist Party solves the "difficult racial problem" by declaring that it must be solved in "Southern style." "Southern style" calls for lynching, segregation, mob terrorism, and the worst forms of persecution and extra exploitation of the Negro poor farmers and agricultural laborers

The *Jewish Forward*, organ of the Socialist Party in New York, printed the usual lie of all lynchers that "Negroes have a weakness for white women." Such malicious propaganda against the Negro proves conclusively that the Socialist Party is against the unity of the Negro and white workers in the struggle for the liberation movement of the Negro masses. It proves that this party is not different than the other two bosses' parties. It likewise endorses lynching. It spreads the same vile propaganda of terrorist organizations as the agents of the two major political parties.

Norman Thomas, the leader of the Socialist Party, on his tour of the South spoke not once to the Negroes but only to the "lily white" respectable business men and "nice" people. Such is the platform of the Socialist Party, for the Negro toilers. It endorses Jim-Crowism, lynchings, mob terrorism and all forms of persecution against the Negro masses.

A. Philip Randolph, president of the Brotherhood of Sleeping Car Porters, a Negro spokesman, is better known for his treacherous sell-out of the Pullman porters. When the majority of the porters voted to strike, Randolph and Green, president of the American Federation of Labor, refused to give leadership, but told the porters to wait. Likewise Randolph accepted a federal charter from the Jim Crow A.F. of L. for the union. This charter does not make the porters union a national organization of the A.F. of L., but an isolated Jim-Crow.

Union With Local Rights

Negro reformist organizations, i.e., The National Association for the Advancement of Colored People, the Urban League, The Interracial Organization, etc., have failed miserably to give the oppressed Negro masses a program of action. Their feeble solution to lynchings and to the economic problems do not rally the rank and file Negro toilers for a decisive struggle. Their program is one to appeal in a humanitarian way to the white ruling class, the breeders of these dastardly crimes, to legislate against these barbarous acts. They fail to see that as long as the white "boss" class can keep the Negro and white workers divided to exploit the working class and wring greater profits from their hides, so long will lynchings and other forms of persecution continue. The organizations are the misleaders of the Negro masses. They are objectively the agents of the white ruling class. They too exploit and betray the masses of Negro toilers with their fake programs. They are working to maintain a mere handful of intellectual exploiters.

The only force that will smash mob terrorism and put an end to lynchings and all forms of segregation is the united struggle of the Negro and white workers. This united front of the working class, struggling against the oppressors of the Negro masses is the most decisive factor to assure a successful destruction of lynchings.

An extensive enlightenment and agitational campaign must be conducted among that section of backward white workers in the South who are corrupted with white "boss" race ideology, to win them to support the struggles of the Negro masses. The most advanced section of white workers recognize the fact that segregation, terrorism and lynchings keep the workers separated and enable the bosses to secure unhampered oppression and exploitation of the working class. Also that racial division of the working class is a factor that lowers the standards of living of the working class and in the South creates the basis for lowering the economic standards of the white workers. The most advanced of these white workers will support the struggles of the Negro mass against lynching and create a genuine united front of all exploited masses against the exploiters.

The backward white workers of the South must be won. The struggle against lynching is the struggle of the working class against the boss class, which struggle requires the solidarity of the Negro toilers and white workers against the white ruling class. This united front will sweep into and discard those disruptive ideas deeply rooted in the American working class that divide the black and white workers.

Negroes are not lynched because they are black. As an oppressed group of people, the white ruling class has succeeded in super exploiting them. The master class has sponsored a program of hatred. It has filled the minds of the white working class with the false and vicious theory of "race" ideology. This false conception has prevented the black and white forces from combining their forces to struggle against the inhuman exploitation by the master class. This super exploitation and barbarous oppression can only be carried on when black and white workers are divided. The bosses must reap more and more profits. They must build more fortunes. But once the entire working class becomes conscious of its positions and tasks, this division will be transformed into an impenetrable front of black and white workers who will fight against the oppression of the Negroes.

Organized mass struggle is the final solution to the oppression and prosecution of the Negro mass.

American Negro Labor Congress

The American Negro Labor Congress is an organization of Negro toilers and white workers. It conducts a merciless struggle against the oppression and persecution of the Negro masses. It unites the black and white workers in a common struggle against social oppression.

The American Negro Labor Congress fights against all forms of white ruling class terrorism, lynching, segregation, and discrimination. It boldly exposes the Jim-Crow policies of the American Federation of Labor which aids employers to super exploit Negro toilers by deliberately refusing to organize this section of labor. The A. F. of L. bars Negro workers from membership from many unions and discriminates against the few that are admitted.

The American Negro Labor Congress organizes the black and white workers on self-defense against the white ruling class. Simultaneously it exposes the middle class of Negro leaders who have betrayed the Negro masses and whose leadership has been one of treachery, compromise and sell-out.

The American Negro Labor Congress wages a campaign for full equality and the right of self-determination of the Negro masses in those areas where they are the majority of the population. Certain areas of the South where the black population is greater than the white, the Negroes should have the right if they choose, to establish their own power, they should rule themselves.

At present the organization is conducting a campaign against lynching. The culmination of this campaign will be the National Convention of American Negro Congress in St. Louis, November 15th-16th. Delegates from the South where economic misery and political oppression and social persecution are more keenly felt will be in attendance. The Congress calls upon the Negro masses and white workers to rally to the support of the A. N. L. C. in the fight against lynching and make the Convention an historical event in the national Negro liberation movement.

Forward to a mass convention! Down With Mob Terrorism!

Organize Workers Defense! For Full Social, Economic, Political Equality of the Negro Masses! For the right of Self-Determination! Join the American Negro Labor Congress!

CHAPTER 2
EARLY NEWSPAPER ARTICLES

To The Exploited and Oppressed
Negro Toilers.
Close Ranks! Join The Communist Party!
[Daily Worker, 1931]

The American working class is faced with a severe economic crisis. Twelve million people are wholly without employment. Forty million persons are without a means of livelihood and other millions are working part time, barely making enough to exist on. Wages are being slashed daily. The hours of working are lengthened. The speed-up system increases. The government and police terror against the toiling masses becomes more brutal and barbarous. As the crisis deepens the militancy of the workers is reflected in strike struggles which the bosses and their government attempt to crush in terror and blood.

In this savage offensive of the bosses to get out of the crisis the Negro toilers are the worst sufferers. The political reaction of the bourgeoisie against the Negroes takes its sharpest form. They systematically violate their own laws (democratic rights, 13th, 14th, and 15th amendments) with the rope and faggot of lynch mobs, with the torrents of legal lynching and the horrors of Jim Crow laws to drive into the lowest depths of economic and political despair the Negro masses. Every organized and unorganized attempt of the Negro masses to resist the tightening yoke of oppression is met with lynchings, lynch frame-ups, shooting down by uniform thugs and semi-feudal terror from the capitalists, their henchmen, and fascist organizations.

The struggle of the Negro masses for liberation at every hand is met by the cold steel of the white ruling class landlords and capitalists. In the Black Belt of the South, American "democracy" enslaves close to nine million Negroes on peonage and share cropping farms. Every elemental democratic right guaranteed by the federal constitution is consistently denied the Negro masses. Chain gang, debt slavery, convict labor, whippings, medieval torture, the multiple horrors accompanying tenancy and peonage, midnight rides of "pure blood Americans" (Ku Klux Klan, American Legion, Black Shirts, etc.) and increase lynchings, spell in capital letters "DEMOCRACY" endorsed and condoned by every political and reactionary body, black and white, except the Communists and the revolutionary organizations of struggle.

The iron clutch of American imperialism which holds in subjection the Negro masses can be broken. Equal rights for the Negroes in the North and national self-determination for the majority of the Negro population in the Black Belt can be gotten but only thru revolutionary struggles under the leadership of the Communist Party.

The programs of the reformists and misleaders turn the militant struggles of the Negro masses into channels not harmful to the imperialists and their agents. Every avenue of escape from the barbarous yoke of oppression becomes a road, under reactionary reformist leadership, to carry the ruling minority class to a fortress of safety guarded by their Cossacks and thugs, armed to the teeth, to plunder and rob the toilers and to drown in blood the growing struggles of the Negro masses.

The Communist party is the leader of the struggles of the workers against the savage political reaction of the bourgeoisie. The party is the leader in the fight against unemployment, mass wage cuts, of the worsening conditions of the toilers and against the immediate war danger. It mobilized the workers, black and white, to stubbornly resist the attempts of the bosses to drive them into another war to slaughter their brother workers in order to prolong the rule of the reigning parasites over the laboring masses. It is the leader of all oppressed national minority groups in the colonial countries, the West Indies and America, against the iron rule of the imperialist bosses.

The recruiting campaign of the Central Committee of the Communist Party, U.S.A. is a drive to bring into the fighting ranks of the workers larger numbers of Negroes and whites, native and foreign born, to give mass resistance to the increased political reaction of the imperialists against the toiling masses.

Negro toilers, this is your Party! Join its ranks! Build a fighting solidarity of Negro and white workers! Build the Negro liberation movement!

In the struggle against lynching it is only the Communists who are actively engaged in mobilizing masses of workers, white and black, to protest and demonstrate against this barbarous pastime of the American bosses.

The struggle to free the nine framed Scottsboro boys, the orphan Jones case, etc. and major political campaigns of the Party to draw into the mass defense movement and into the ranks of the Negro liberation movement thousands of white workers to struggle together with the Negroes against oppression. In Camp Hill, Ala., the determined struggles of the Negro share croppers against the starvation plans of the plantation bosses were supported by the Communist Party. In the struggle against unemployment and the mass eviction of Negro workers (Chicago and Cleveland) Communists were actively engaged in building up the mass movement which forced the capitalists of the cities to give certain amounts of relief to the Negro jobless. The National Hunger March to Washington, D.C. of 1,650, of which a fourth were Negroes, proved the vitality of the Communist program of full equality for the Negro in smashing Jim Crow barriers all along the lines of march and in the Capital. Recent strikes of the miners in Kentucky, Pennsylvania, Ohio, and West Virginia, proved conclusively the correctness of the Communist program of unity of black and white in strike struggles to force concessions from the coal barons.

The only solution to the wretched conditions of the Negro masses is the Communist program of struggle—full equality for the Negroes in the North can be obtained only after a relentless struggle of the black and white proletariat against the bourgeoisie. The right of national self-determination for the Negroes in the Black Belt can be realized by revolutionary struggles, with the white workers in the forefront, by the confiscation of the land properties of the Southern big landlords; by taking the power away from the imperialists (who use it to suppress the Negro majority in the Black Belt) and placing it in the hands of the Black workers and peasants.

For unconditional equal rights of the Negro masses! For the right of national self-determination of the Negro population which is the majority in the Black Belt of the South! Close ranks with the advanced sections of the white workers! Join the Communist Party—the Party of your class!

Negro Workers Are Hard Hit By Unemployment; Must Organize
[*Daily Worker*, 1930]

That terrible scourge of the working class, unemployment, is most keenly felt by the masses of Negro workers. The percentage of unemployment in the large industrial centers, in proportion to the population, averages between 25 per cent and 33 1-3 per cent among Negroes, according to an official statement of the crusader news agency.

In Cincinnati, the Negro population is one tenth of the total population but according to the figures of the chamber of commerce the Negroes who are unemployed are one third of the total number of jobless.

In Chicago, out of a half million of unemployed workers, 25 per cent are Negroes. In the smaller industrial cities the rate of unemployment among Negroes averages 33 1-3 per cent.

The deepness of unemployment is best illustrated by the number of evictions which take place in the Negro territories. In Baltimore, fifteen evictions of Negro families took place in less than three weeks. However, all these families returned to their homes to the heroic work of the Unemployed Councils which gathered the workers in the neighborhood to return the furniture. During the month of January, over a thousand evictions took place in the city of New York, out of which number were over three hundred Negro families.

Another evidence of hard times and misery suffered by the Negro workers is the breadlines. In the Negro centers of cities like New York, Chicago, etc., hundreds of Negro men and women clog the breadlines daily. Because of the inhuman treatment received, standing out in the cold for hours waiting for their measly rations, shoved and bullied by potbellied lackeys of the police department, the Negro workers in the Harlem breadline smashed the headquarters of the Salvation Army Relief station. This latter bosses' institution, aside from giving out food that was fit only for the garbage, treated the workers as if they were savage leopards.

During the early part of the year, the twins of a Negro family in Brooklyn died from starvation. These children were killed by the bosses who breed unemployment and continually drive the living conditions of the workers to the lowest level, while they themselves live in luxury.

In England, Arkansas, 500 Negro and white poor farmers marched into the town and demanded bread for their starving families. These poor farmers live in the Delta region which could not grow crops because of the drought. An attempt of a lawyer-plantation owner to quiet these starved farmers, who had become enraged by their miserable conditions, was defeated. The poor farmers were determined to get food for their families or fight. The small store keepers called upon the Red Cross, who doled out $2.75 of provisions.

In Oklahoma City, the Negro and white workers, tired of waiting upon relief that was not coming, smashed a merchant's store and took the food that they needed.

This severe unemployment crisis reaches out into every territory. Negro and white agricultural workers have left the farms in large numbers. In one month a southern railroad company sold, in two counties, over one hundred and seventy tickets. Many of these farm laborers do not have money to buy railroad tickets and are compelled to beat their way to the cities. Here they can not find work and add to the already large numbers of unemployed. Large masses of Negro toilers and rural districts are facing starvation. But they refuse to starve. They are organizing and must continue to organize into fighting groups, demanding unemployment insurance and food from the local and state governments.

A.N.L.C. As Mass Organization of Negro Workers

[*Daily Worker*, June 13, 1930]

The economic crisis that has a firm hold in the U.S.A. has keenly affected the 12,000,000 Negro workers. The crisis, with mass unemployment and wage cuts, is far reaching among the Negro poor farmers, agricultural laborers, and workers. It has been plainly shown that the first to receive lay-offs, wage cuts, and evictions from their homes are the Negro workers. Those who are working have the most menial jobs, laboring under intolerable conditions and working long hours. This economic pressure is driving the Negro workers into the revolutionary wave. Among the rank and file there is a fast growing realization that this oppression caused by the capitalist system of inhuman exploitation that can be combated only thru struggle. More and more, they are organizing into groups to throw off the yoke of their oppressors. But in most instances the leaders of these groups have proven false and have betrayed the workers into the hands of the bosses. Many of these organizations have been without a clear understanding as to the real cause of the deep-growing crisis.

The Negro workers are doubly exploited, both as Negroes and as workers. They are in an unorganized state. The A. F. of L. has made no attempt to organize these workers. A few Jim Crow locals have been set up and discrimination is practiced in others. In this way the reactionary trade unions serve their bosses by pitting one group of workers against another. Dividing white workers and Negro workers, using the latter as scab labor in many instances, keeps wages low and causes hatred which prevents organizing. In direct contrast to this method of the A. F. of L., the T.U.U.L. has a program of struggle for Negro and white workers alike. It organizes both on the same basis into the same union and vigorously fights against all forms of race hatred.

The reformist organizations, such as the National Association for the Advancement of Colored People, the Urban League, etc., have failed miserably to give the Negro masses a program of action. Their feeble solution to the economic problems of today does not rally support from the rank and file Negro workers. These false leaders do not understand the basic cause of the crisis, since their interests are not in common with interests of the workers, and they help to perpetuate the capitalist system of hatred between black and white workers. Neither do they understand that the recent waves of lynching are a part of the capitalist system to perpetuate hatred between the black and white workers.

The need of a broad mass organization for the Negro masses is quite apparent. Such a working class organization must have a program of struggle and must enlighten and develop the Negro worker to resist the growing offensive of the bosses. The millions of rank and file Negro workers who know of the class struggle but are not conscious, must be reached. These unorganized workers engaged in the basic industries are good potential elements for a mass organization. Such movements as the Garvey clubs must be penetrated further. In this organization, the rank and file have become somewhat militant. Yet they have been deceived by false and corrupt leadership. This leadership which built visionary dreams of a return to Africa which would be the establishment of a Negro Imperialism, has robbed the Negro masses of millions of dollars. It has not given them a program of struggle, but in its place a dream that can't come true.

The Garvey movement does not put forth the establishment of a workers' and farmers' government as in the Soviet Union. A return to Africa if possible, would mean the inhuman exploitation of the Negro masses by a newly created Negro bourgeoisie. This would come about because of the pressure brought to compete with the other imperialist nations.

The Garvey movement encourages the division of Negro and white workers, so that a few corrupt Negro leaders may exploit the rank and file. The leadership fails to see that only through the solidarity of the Negro and white workers, fighting against their common enemy the bosses, can the oppressed national minorities win their struggles against the bourgeoisies and the right to self-determination as has been done in the Soviet Union.

The A.N.L.C. as a broad mass organization can prepare the Negro masses for greater struggles. It can win a great number of these unorganized workers to our Party by acting as a bridge organization. It can dispel that fear and suspicion of the Negro workers to white comrades and build a united front of Negro and white workers. It must fight for the admittance of Negro workers into trade unions and organize Negro and white workers into industrial unions. It must fight for the right of the masses to have freedom of speech, press, and assemblage. It must fight against all forms of race hatred, segregation, political disfranchisement and for the equal schooling for Negro children.

The masses of Negro workers must be organized for the struggle against international imperialism, they must unite with the colonial, European, and Asiatic workers in their struggles. American imperialist aggression in Mexico, Haiti, Nicaragua, and other colonial countries redoubles the task of the A.N.L.C. A great number of workers who are not ready to accept our Party policy can be brought under the influence of the A.N.L.C. In this organization the Negro workers of the U.S.A. who are more industrialized, can be developed to become leaders of the oppressed colonial Negro masses.

These many tasks can only be achieved through the thorough and energetic work of a mass organization functioning in reality as a bridge between the Negro masses and our Party. The present crisis affords our Party the opportunity of greater direct contact with Negro masses through a broad A.N.L.C.

Fight Against Garveyism
[*Daily Worker*, June 25, 1930]

The masses of Negro workers in the U.S.A. and other colonial countries who have been super-exploited for centuries by the white ruling class, read-ily gave an ear to the *"fluent"* and *"eloquent"* phrases of Marcus Garvey about ten years ago. Garvey came at a time when the masses were seething with discontent.

The Negro workers, fooled into entering into the world war, gave their blood to help maintain capitalism. But the effect of going to other imperialist countries had its reaction among the Negro workers. Treated and adored as heroes abroad because they were loyal fighters, fighting for what they knew not, the Negro workers expected upon their return home to be given better consideration. Because they had helped to maintain capitalist democracy, they expected to be served as true sons of a supposed democratic republic. But instead, segregation, the worst forms of raced hatred, lynchings and open insults (while still in uniform) greeted them. The result was that the labor hating bosses who breed lynchings, segregation, etc., to keep the workers divided laid the fire for race riots'which occur throughout the country.

Close to these events came Garvey with his visionary plans to establish a nation in Africa to protect Negro workers and to build large Negro enter-prises to give employment to Negroes. How could this dream come true? Only through an extensive collection of millions of dollars. At first Garvey aroused the militant spirit in the masses; he planted the seed of revolution. But when he began to organize segregated visions, put on a dues paying ba-sis with he and his sub officials receiving a majority of the finances, he changed the revolutionary program. In place of a program of struggle he substituted one to make peace. He became reactionary.

Preachers Fleece Workers

Jack-leg preachers and many worthless characters with smooth-flowing tongues were given an opportunity to fleece the rank and file workers. All kinds of illusions were advanced. Property must be bought, business enter-prises started and trade with oppressed colonial countries for which ships were purchased, had to be established. Not to be excluded were the enor-mous salaries of the newly-created officials. The entire machinery was oiled and set in motion.

Two hundred million dollars was collected and squandered by the crooks. Today the leaders of the organization are asking for the vast sum of $600,000,000. The result is that the members have become dissatisfied. Split after split has occurred.

At the convention last summer in Jamaica many attended with the idea that a general house cleaning would take place. But Garvey supported the crooks by keeping them in office.

Garvey Takes Advantage of Exploited People

How plainly does this reveal that Garvey is a petty bourgeois adventurer, taking advantage of exploited people. The theory of establishing a black republic as well as the opportunism of Garvey must be exposed by our Party. Some of his followers are sincere in believing that the establishing of Africa as a home to protect Negro workers, would bring freedom. This is not true. If the Negro masses did overthrow the imperialists who at present occupy Africa what would be the result? The establishment of a proletarian dictatorship as in the Soviet Union? No! But the establishing of a nation such as Liberia or Cuba. These republics are directly dominated by American imperialism. The masses are bitterly exploited to support the American bankers and industrialists, who have connived with the treacherous home landers to acquire large tracts of land thereby robbing the natives. In return the natives must work on these lands at starvation wages. In Cuba the native misleaders have agreed with the American imperialists to hunt down and kill all those who attempt to organize the peasants into militant organizations, such as the Communists.

The most severe oppression, just as sharp as now, if not sharper, would come and the Negro workers would awaken to find themselves forced to fight against a newly formed Negro bourgeoisie. Garveyism is a retreat away from the struggle for liberty of the Negro masses. It proposes to find a way to compromise with the imperialists. It is reactionary and not revolutionary and has given up the fight for national aspiration of the Negro masses. Liberty cannot come through such channels, it can only come through struggle. To quote Marx: "Labor in the white skin cannot free itself as long as labor in the black skin is branded." This means that the uniting of the exploited Negro and white workers to fight against their common enemy, the capitalist class, is the only solution for liberty. Not one section of labor can be free itself as long as another section remains in chains. You must fight also to free your brother worker.

Garveyism preaches hatred of white workers by Negro workers. It teaches the separate division of the working class. To antagonize Negro workers against white workers is wrong. An educational and enlightenment campaign must be waged among the Negro and white workers to teach them solidarity. The ignorant white workers must be taught that they must unite with the exploited black workers to break the chains of capitalist exploitation. They must be taught that the hatred which they have for one another is created by the bosses' policy to perpetuate the enslaving of the exploited masses.

The slogan put forth by our Party of Self-Determination for the oppressed Negro masses in Africa, Southern U.S.A., the colonial countries, etc., should be popularized among the Garveyites. This slogan is an immediate demand upon the imperialist nations for the Negro masses to set up their own government wherever they form the majority of the population. An outstanding example where the oppressed minorities under the building of socialism have their own government is the Soviet Union. The masses of Negro and white workers must join the Communist Party and the revolutionary Trade Union Unity League and fight shoulder to shoulder for the complete emancipation of the entire working class.

Vote Communist—Negro Workers!
[*Daily Worker*, September 5, 1930]

Immediately after the Civil War the Negro toilers were given bourgeois democratic rights by the 13th, 14th and 15th amendments to the United States constitution. This enactment gave the former slaves full suffrage and the right to hold parliamentary office. For the first time, the Negro workers were given equal rights; they became the allies of the Northern industrial capitalists.

But this freedom did not last long. The Northern industrial bourgeoisie, intent in their purposes to crush the Southern slave-holders, so they could proceed, unhampered, to gain state power for the free development of capitalism and to establish the rule of the industrial bourgeoisie, soon deserted the Negro workers. Friendly relations were established between the Northern and Southern bourgeoisie and the propertyless Negro toilers who had been granted equal rights had them taken away and were forced to return to their former slave masters, who reduced them to the state of semi-slavery. This was accomplished in the name of the "great Republican party," "the party of Lincoln," the "Emancipator."

Organizations Crush Negro Toilers

Obviously there arose in the South various organizations which attempted to perpetuate the traditional conditions of the master and slave. Such were the Ku Klux Klan and the Democratic Party under the leadership of the dastardly reactionary politicians.

With an unwritten agreement, the two major political parties simultaneously pursued parallel courses leading to the same goal, the development of industrial capital through the super-exploitation of the entire working class. It was evident that all attempts at organization among the Negro workers and whites would be difficult. Consequently a wily and careful plan of poisonous propaganda was put in motion. This propaganda was to spread hatred in its most bitter forms among the Negro and white workers.

The two major political parties are not concerned about the conditions of the workers, but about making greater profits for their bosses. The politicians for the Republican and Democratic parties are the true lackeys of "Gerard's 64 parasites." They must legislate to protect their bosses who are interested only in making more and more profits.

These lackeys have betrayed the Negro workers time and time again. They have enforced lynchings, segregation, disfranchisement, mob-terrorism and all forms of persecution against the Negro toilers. Whenever the Negro workers became dissatisfied and began to talk of rebelling these "pot-licking" agents appeased their irritated feelings by selecting the most despicable lackey among the Negro petty bourgeoisie and placing him in some official position.

The demands and grievances, in so far as the workers are concerned, have only been granted to the extent of quieting the rising spirit of revolt in the masses and endeavoring to cause them to forget their miserable plight and exploitation.

In this manner, the Negro workers have been the football of bourgeois politicians.

Socialist Party

The Socialist Party, a worthy contemporary of the other two bourgeois democratic organizations, cloaked in deceptive progressive phrases, has not a platform for the Negro workers. Its leadership endorses the brutal crushing of spirit and beatings of workers who fight for workers' demands. The leadership of the Socialist Party consists of those right wing elements that support finance capital. The left wing, the more radical group, split away over ten years ago and formed what is now the Communist Party of America.

Communist Party and Negro Workers

The Communist Party election platform exposes the misleaders of labor in the American Federation of Labor, the Socialist Party and other parties. In fact, it pulls the cover off the entire capitalist system, showing that a new war is in the making and that the imperialist powers are attempting to attack the Soviet Union. The platform demands immediate and adequate unemployment relief and introduces an unemployment insurance bill for the workers, the funds for which are to be supplied from the surplus profits of the bosses.

It advocates the building of revolutionary trade unions and wages a fight for the repeal of all criminal syndicalism, anarchist and sedition laws. The platform states that "anti Negro laws are the most vicious anti-labor laws" and "to stop lynching, the rule of the white bourgeoisie must be ended."

The Communist Party demands the right of self-determination for the Negro masses where the Negroes are the majority.

The struggle against race discrimination, against lynching and against persecution of every description must be the concern of the entire working class of the United States. As long as the bosses succeed in pitting white workers against black workers, it will be impossible to pit the whole working class against the capitalist class. Support of any form of race prejudice, therefore, is anti-labor and is support of capitalism itself.

The Communist Party is the best political fighter for the Negro workers. It demands and fights for complete social and political equality for the Negro toilers. The Negro workers and farmers must support the Party of their class. They must support the candidates of the Communist Party. Negro workers and farmers! In the South and North, vote Communist!

Marion Demonstrates American Democracy
[*Daily Worker*, August 14, 1930]

The latest outstanding example of "American democracy" and liberty for the Negro workers was demonstrated to the American Negroes last week in Marion, Ind.. Marion, before practically unknown, overnight had its name blazoned upon the front pages of the bourgeois press and sealed in the blood of two Negro workers, became the "exponent of American democracy," and the chief rival of Texas, Georgia, Mississippi, Oklahoma, etc. Simultaneously, it joined the southern states and voiced its approval of attempting to perpetuate "white (boss) supremacy" through lynching and mob terrorism.

American Democracy and the Negro Workers

The American Negro workers have been the footstool of bourgeois society ever since the first boat load of slaves landed on the shores of Virginia in 1619. From the sweat and blood of these workers, American capitalism has made its base of super and inhuman exploitation. The Negroes are exploited as workers and are oppressed as a national minority. As workers they first feel the sharpness of the economic crisis. They are the first to lose their jobs and receive evictions from their homes. The most menial jobs are given these workers who receive the lowest pay and work the longest hours. The fascist and social fascist leadership of the American Federation of Labor has never been concerned to organize these workers. Only here and there through the initiative of misleaders of the labor movement or reformists have a few Jim-Crow locals been established. And these have never taken up the grievances of the Negro workers nor presented a militant program of action whereby their barbarous conditions could be bettered.

As a national minority the oppression is more keenly felt. The white ruling class pursues a conscious and deliberate policy of spreading the germ of race hatred among all workers. Through the text books and schools, the churches and theaters, the press and radio, a veritable breastwork of poisonous propaganda is built. Yearly tons of literatures pronounce the Negro worker as inferior. Segregation, discrimination, lynching, mob terrorism and the worst forms of persecution are the lot of the Negro workers. Not alone are the "Gold Star Mothers" Jim-Crowed, but in the jails and prisons this damnable practice is carried on so efficiently to the extent of provoking race wars.

Through this carefully planned system of propaganda, the bosses kindle the fire for race riots and through lynching attempt to keep up hatred among the Negro and white workers. Thereby the ranks of the workers are split and organization is rendered difficult. This is done to prevent the building of united fronts of rank and file workers fighting against the real enemy, the capitalist class.

As long as the capitalist system of society endures, so long will there be "festivals" as was held in Marion. An escape from the South to North or to Africa is not the solution to the Negro problem. The semi-feudal oppression in the South has its counterpart in a highly intensified industrial exploitation in the North. In Africa and the colonial countries, imperialism has developed the most barbarous system of chattel slavery. To the Negro workers "democracy" is an unknown term.

To smash mob terrorism, to fight against lynching, and race hatred, requires the solidarity of Negro and white workers united in a common struggle against the main enemy, capitalism.

The revolutionary Negro liberation movement is supported by the fullest realization of the class-conscious white workers that capitalism attempts to retain racial subjection in order to perpetuate the exploitation and oppression of the entire working class. Sharp struggles, lynchings, race wars, economic and race discrimination against the Negroes are methods used by the boss class to lower the conditions of the white workers. The demonstrative solidarity of Negro and white workers fighting for social, economic and political equality for the Negro workers is a factor that will gather the Negro workers to become the natural allies of the world revolutionary proletariat. Only through such a united force, exterminating capitalism and all its outgrowths (lynchings, unemployment, economic crises, and white chauvinism) and in its place establishing a rule of the workers and peasants will such debacles as took place in Marion disappear. The liberation struggle of the American working class involves the liberation movement of the Negro workers.

The Communist Party, the vanguard of the working class, leads in organizing both Negro and white workers for struggle against all forms of oppression and persecution. It is the Communist Party that raises the slogan of self-determination, the highest expression of equality, for the Negro masses. The Communist Party through struggle will win the American proletariat to struggle for the national aspirations of the Negro workers. Under the leadership of the Communist Party, the Negro workers will assume the hegemony of the Negro liberation movement.

Fight Against White Chauvinism
[*Daily Worker*, December 10, 1930]

The majority of Negro toilers, after hearing about self-determination of the Negro majorities in the Black Belt, readily agree that our line is correct. The establishing of a correct political line on the Negro question and our efforts to put this line into application has brought under our influence thousands of Negro toilers. But there is a sharp disparity between our influence and our organizational advances. It is well to make a thorough examination and discover some of our weaknesses.

We are agreed that our political line is correct. But have we positively convinced the Negro toilers of this fact? Do they believe that we are sincere? Have we energetically attempted to eradicate their distrust? Have our enlightenment campaigners among the white and Negro workers been sustained and persistent? To these questions we must give the negative answer, No!

The existence of such burning questions give concrete evidence for the cause of such alarming disparity and suspicion. One of the most fundamental reasons for this condition is white chauvinism. This vitriolic, capitalist, venom as yet pervades the minds of vast sections of the white American working class and can be found in a semi-dormant stage among few Party members, union members, and sympathizers.

Bourgeois Prejudice in Action

Recently, several Negro workers attended a dance at the Finnish Workers Club in New York. The presence of these dark skinned workers was objectionable to certain non-class conscious elements. An attempt, on the part of these hooligans, was made to eject the Negroes. In a mild manner their plans were thwarted and the Negroes remained.

In the Lithuanian Cooperative restaurant in Chicago this "white superiority" cropped out in a bold manner at the unemployed workers convention. The "comrades" of the restaurant refused to feed the Negro delegates, giving as the pretext that it would hurt their business. They suggested and did give to the Negroes money in order that they could eat somewhere else.

At the Russian Cooperative restaurant in Gary a stubborn policy was carried thru in refusing to employ Negro workers. One was hired, but at a meeting of the board a vote was taken and the majority vote of the white chauvinists discharged the worker.

Also in this same city it is reported that the Party section organizer slandered and ridiculed the Negro leadership in the Y.C.L. This organizer made statements that Negro work is no more important than any other kind of work and that Negro comrades should only do Negro work. He gave the vicious lie that Negro comrades in Gary joined the Party for special privileges and accused them falsely of importing white girl comrades from Chicago for a dance.

In the Needle Trades Union, the officialdom fails to recognize the necessity of doing special work among the 15,000 Negro needle trades workers in New York. In some of our union shops, Negro workers receive lower wages than the whites for the same kind of work, but the shop committee does not think it important to pull a strike and fight for equal pay for equal work for the Negro union members. Our comrades stated that the Negro workers are not discriminated against in the industry, they only receive lower wages.

Methods of Work

Such crass manifestations of white chauvinism create Herculean obstacles that rightfully cause the Negro toilers to be suspicious of the White Communists, our program and unions and remain on the fringe of the movement. We have not conducted a broad and intensified educational campaign in our press and organizations. Our best efforts have been all too feeble. It has been stated that we have not jumped at the throats of these one hundred per cent Americans. There is no place in the movement, Party and unions, etc. for such elements, who by their action contribute to the support of American capitalist oppression of the Negro masses.

It is not enough to pass resolutions of protest a week later, after the deed is done and the culprits have gone some place else to continue their dirt. It is insufficient to have a Negro speaker come later to speak on the Negro question and thunderously applaud him. Mild criticisms and slow action to condemn white chauvinism do not demonstrate to the Negro toilers that we are sincere in assuming the hegemony of the Negro liberation movement.

But at the time the act is committed, the Communists and members of the revolutionary trade unions must openly brand and expose those one hundred per centers. We must conduct a tenacious, systematic, and consistent fight against this Yankee arrogance, which combined with social antagonisms creates special forms of national and social oppression under which the Negro masses endure great hardship.

The Communists attending the Finnish dance, should have instantly stopped the dance and exposed the racial chauvinism which is capitalist ideology deeply rooted in the American working class. A thirty minute educational talk should have been given, denouncing the rowdies and calling upon the workers to pass a protest resolution to be published in the Finnish press and other press. Wide circulation could have been given the resolution. Many protest meetings should have been held condemning bourgeois prejudices and hooliganism. These same tactics should have been applied in the Lithuanian and Russian Cooperatives.

Our leadership cannot retain polluted functionaries. Unless they make a sincere repudiation and energetically set about to purge themselves of bureaucracism and white superiority, they must be expelled. Words of confession mean little, but daily deeds and actions will convince and win the Negro toilers to struggle with the white class conscious proletariat for full equality. In the Party and press these functionaries must be exposed. A persistent barrage must be directed against them. They should be placed on trial before a workers' court and ruthlessly prosecuted by white and Negro workers. At mass meetings of the workers these elements must be stigmatized for what they are. Special series of meetings discussing the subject must be held.

Role of Negro Masses

Only such methods of work will win the Negro toilers for our revolutionary unions and Party, thereby closing the gap between our tremendous influence and organizational gains.

The Negro masses are a huge reservoir of dynamic revolutionary material. If we fail to realize this, we fail to understand the class struggle and the important role that these potential allies of the white revolutionary proletariat will play.

We fail to see the growing restlessness of black toilers throughout the world. Our task is to assist them in their efforts to gain freedom. We must help mould this revolutionary upsurge into a fighting confederacy of white and Negro workers for the great struggles that lurk in the near future. We must destroy white chauvinism, branch and root, to achieve this aim.

Opportunism on March 28
[*Daily Worker*, April 10, 1931]

The sharp offensive of the imperial bosses, their drives against the foreign-born workers, and the all-around sharpening of the yoke of persecution against the laboring masses, made March 28 an important day in the history of the toiling masses.

Recognizing these facts, this day was set aside as the national day of protest against lynching, discrimination, and deportations. The Party's fractions in the League of Struggle for Negro Rights, the International Labor Defense, and the Council for Protection of the Foreign-Born were instructed to mobilize the membership and all other available forces. All district organizations of the Party received detailed instructions and a model plan as a guide for making preparations. The results were so far from the mass character that they should have attained, that we were obliged to assume that little or no preparations were made by the district organizations. Recent examination of the work of four of the largest districts of the Party by the Political Bureau, have shown that the assumption was correct.

It is quite evident that the comrades underestimated the importance of this solidarity campaign, and instead of the districts actually taking hold and mobilizing the forces at their disposal to assist the three organizations which had the leadership of the demonstration, the entire work was relegated to one or two comrades of the League of Struggle for Negro Rights and maybe the International Labor Defense and the Council for the Protection of the Foreign-Born.

What meetings and marches were held, have not been reported to the *Daily Worker* or to the Central Office. There was a total lack of cooperation and insufficient preparation. The disorganized manner in which the few meetings that we have received reports on, were conducted, is an indication of the necessity of changing our methods of work.

Never before in the history of our Party have we had such a favorable situation to arouse the indignation of the masses of Negro workers and foreign-born workers, as we have today, to protest against the persecution directed against them. Much as the comrades are aware of these facts, yet we notice that there was manifested an unconscious reluctance to supply the motivating power for the success of our solidarity campaigns. It is little short of criminal neglect that the demonstrations of March 28 were a failure.

Regardless of the results of these demonstrations, the comrades are instructed to immediately send in the reports from the outlying sections and districts, whether meetings preparing for the 28th were held, and on the activities of the 28th itself.

To create mass action among the Negro and white workers against the terrific and savage persecutions of the toiling masses, it is necessary to build up mass sentiment for struggle, through successful mobilization of native and foreign-born, Negro and white workers to demonstrate their solidarity and their willingness to give stubborn resistance to capitalist persecution and starvation. All manifestations of under-estimating the significance of this work, all passive reluctance to mobilize masses of workers for participation in meetings and demonstrations, all tendencies to relegate to a handful comrades the struggle to build united fronts, must be sharply combated and condemned. Methods of work that were used in the March 28 demonstration are opportunistic and have no place in the revolutionary movement.

The revolutionary organizations must purge themselves from all passivity and irresponsible slip-shod routine methods (which objectively give support to the enemy) of conducting national campaigns of solidarity. Sectarian propaganda methods do not meet the requirements of the present period. Carefully planned, mass agitational methods are adapted to this period to assure maximum results. Well organized, systematic and energetic campaigns must be put into force; masses of Negro workers and white workers must be mobilized to voice their dissatisfaction with, and fight against the existing reign of terror directed against the working class, especially the Negroes and foreign-born.

We are responsible to give real and conscious leadership to this movement.

Smash the Enemy Breastworks!
[*Daily Worker*, October 10, 1931]

In order to perpetrate their system of robbery and exploitation of the Negro masses, the white ruling class has spread its poisonous fangs of hatred among the groups of the white laboring class. "This breastwork" of defense which keeps the Negro and white workers divided, rendering organization more difficult contributes to the deepening of racial antagonisms. Likewise it prevents a netted attack against the boss class by the masses of workers to better their living conditions.

The revolutionary trade unions must recognize the necessity of winning the majority of the working class to support the right for better economic conditions. To win the confidence of the Negro workers for participation in the struggle, to smash the white superiority complex and 100 per cent Yankee arrogance, is a cardinal task of the trade unions. To achieve this end we must ever be on the alert to destroy the bulwark of white chauvinism, and all manifestations of passivity and resistance to demonstrate to the Negro workers the correctness of our program of struggle.

Recently in the Needle Trades Union in Philadelphia, the comrades had an opportunity to prove to the Negro workers the correctness of the union line towards all workers. But they did not avail themselves of this convenient occasion. At a dance given by the custom tailor group, several Negro workers attempted to buy tickets to the affair, but were persuaded not to go into the hall as their presence might bring an objection from some attending the dance. Because one of the Negroes did not evidence a spirit to fight and test the attitude of the Yankee arrogates, the comrade offered this as an excuse for not waging a desperate fight immediately. The organizer of the union took the floor and made a speech, failing to mention the exclusion of the

Negroes, but merely explaining the program of the Trade Union Unity League on the Negro question. This he thought to be sufficient and would break down the opposition. But the Negro workers who remained at the door were not brought in until the talk was over. Fear of trouble between the white workers, poisoned by boss ideology, and Negro workers, would break up the dance was the pretext given preventing drastic action.

Such methods will not destroy white chauvinism, but contribute to the support of prolonging the fight and more firmly entrench the capitalist class in its position to separate the workers and exact huge profits from their labor. The comrades en mass should have torn the throats of the white chauvinists by ushering in the Negro workers. With the white comrades in the front a vitriolic attack should have been launched against these elements in speeches that were delivered. And, yes, in case of a fight the task of white comrades should have been to have fought bitterly for the complete rout of the one hundred per cent Americans. Passivity and reluctance to carry out at once such a revolutionary program can not be tolerated in our unions. The white comrades must assume the leadership. The unwillingness to enter the hall on the part of the Negro workers is permissible because the white workers have not shown them that they (the white workers) will fight for the right of the Negroes and will not desert them in the times of a crisis.

The revolutionary trade union will not tolerate passivity and resistance to demonstrations that will go a long way toward winning the confidence of the Negro workers. Must less will expressions of white chauvinism be permitted. A campaign must be immediately started in the union of Philadelphia to destroy root and branchism. The District Control Commission has taken a definite step in the direction to smash the breastworks of white chauvinism of the enemy by sharply condemning the incorrect methods of fight of the comrades. The breastworks of the enemy must be smashed. It can be done in America just as it was done in the Soviet Union at Stalingrad.

CHAPTER 3
THEORETICAL ESSAYS

The Negro National Oppression and Social Antagonisms

[*The Communist*, March 1931]

"The Negro agricultural laborers and the tenant farmers feel most the pressure of the white persecution and exploitation. Thus the agrarian problem lies at the root of the Negro national movement." (Thesis, Sixth World Congress.)

The Civil War, a struggle between the industrial bourgeoisie of the North and the slave-owners of the South, did not achieve the real emancipation of the slaves. It is true that by an amendment to the federal constitution bourgeois democratic rights were granted, supposedly to guarantee the new freedom. For the first time the Negroes were granted the right to vote, to hold public office, to obtain an equal education, which for a brief period were enforced by Negro militia and northern federal troops.

But the northern bourgeoisie entered into a rapprochement with the overthrown southern plantation lords, thus deserting the property-less former slaves. The northern capitalists were unable to carry the bourgeois-democratic tasks of the war to the end, the taking of the land from the slave holders and giving it to the slaves. If this had been done, the former slaves would not have been forced to return to their former masters after their cowardly betrayal by the northern bourgeoisie, to obtain a livelihood.

Thus the Negro masses in the South, left property-less by their northern "friends," were abandoned to their fate at the hands of their former masters. The former slave-holders soon denied the Negroes their newly granted democratic rights and reduced them to a state of semi-slavery, the plantation system.

Nominal slavery passed away, but the subsequent dependence of the betrayed Negroes upon their previous masters continued the institution in another form. The plantation tenancy system was adopted by the landlords as a means to continue their robbery of the Negro masses, and continued to contribute to the development of industrial capital, in the North and South.

Tenancy

What then is tenancy? *It is a vile abortive means of slavery, successfully enforced by a corrupt social system that is intent in its purpose to crush and subject the Negroes to the South, to facilitate huge profits for the white ruling class and maintain its power over the workers.* Tenants can be divided into 5 classes: 1.) croppers whose work-animals and implements are furnished by the planters; 2.) standing renters who pay a stated amount of farm products for the use of the land and whose implements are usually all furnished with their work-animals; 4.) share cash tenants who pay the rent partly in products and partly in cash and furnish their implements; and 5.) cash tenants who pay entirely cash for the use of the land, furnishing all of their farming equipment.

A notable feature of the tenancy is that the owner supplies not only the land but usually part of the required capital and equipment. In return he receives a share crop. The tenant furnishes all of the labor and occasionally part of the equipment, receiving part of the crop after harvesting.

The standing renters and croppers are the most dependent of all the classes of tenants. The landlords supply them with almost everything and as a result they receive comparatively no returns for their labor. They are so dependent that they know not what liberty is and they are subject altogether to the desire of the landlords, being practically chained to them. It is from the labor of this class of tenants that huge profits are derived. They have no capital with which to pay rent and provide the elementary necessities of life.

Contracts

Conferences are held with the tenants, usually at the beginning or the end of the year. At such a time the tenant agrees to sign a contract which is enforced by the laws of the various Southern States. In many instances the tenants are illiterate. But even if they understand, because of sheer force and intimidation, they sign away the few rights they have.

These contracts are decidedly unfavorable to the tenant. The interpretation of the agreement is always in the hands of the planter, who is assisted by the courts and officers of the law to enforce its terms. The contract always is determined by the desires of the planter. To question the word of a landlord is criminal. The landlords make the laws and either execute them or hire lackeys for the purpose. There is no appeal for the tenant. He is reduced to a serf, or peon.

A typical contract reads in part:

Said tenant further agrees that he violates the contract, or neglects, or abandons or fails (or in the owner's judgment violates this contract or fails) to properly work or cultivate the land early or at proper times, or in case he should become physically or legally incapacitated from working said lands or should die during the term of his lease, or fails to gather or save the crops when made, or fails to pay the rents or advances made by the owner, when due, then in case of full possession of said premises, crops and improvements, in which event this contract may become void and cancelled at the owner's option, and all indebtedness by the tenant for advances or rent shall at once become due and payable to the owner who treats them as due and payable without further notice to the tenant; and the tenant hereby agrees to surrender the quiet and peaceful possession of said premises to the owner at said time, in which event the owner is hereby authorized to transfer, sell or dispose of all property thereon the tenant has any interest in, and in order to entitle the owner to do so, it shall not be necessary to give any notice of any failure or violation of this contract by the tenant, the execution of this lease being sufficient notice of defalcation on the part of the tenant, and shall be so construed by the parties hereto, any law, usage or custom to the contrary notwithstanding.

The terms of such a contract are not only binding, but place the destiny of the tenant completely at the desire of the owner.

Boss Supervision

After the tenant has signed the contract, the landlord sends out a rider whose task is to supervise all the work on the plantations. The boss divides the land among the tenants, giving them a certain amount of fertilizer to use on the acres for cultivation. Also he tells when the crop should be planted. The tenant is forced to start work as soon as there is sufficient light and toil until dark. In the summer the usual starting hour is 4 o'clock. An hour is permitted for lunch. For the wife who works, she is granted two hours for lunch, the extra hour to prepare the meal.

Ordinarily the cropper works from sun-up to sun-down, six days a week.

Division of Profits

Without money with which to pay rent or buy the elementary necessities of life while they are waiting on the maturing, harvesting and selling of the crop, tenants consequently obtain their supplies on credit from the planter or merchant who takes a lien on the crop. This credit system makes it possible for the store keeper or owner to charge exorbitant prices for supplies.

After the crop is harvested and sold, the planter deducts from the profits whatever debt the cropper has contracted during the year. The value of the articles is left solely to the will of the plantation owner, who never figures in the favor of the cropper. The landlord owns in most cases the tools of production, the land, stock, and by an unwritten law, the cropper. Whatever profits are derived from the year's transactions are eaten up by the debts accumulated during the off season, according to the accounting of the landlord. Rarely only does the cropper receive a profit. When he does the amount is so small that it does not better his condition. Thus from one year to another the tenant finds himself in debt to his landlord, who keeps the books and decides the division of profits.

In the South there are upwards of 38,000 plantations averaging about 6 tenants each. In 1925 there were over 625,000 tenants in the South, operating nearly 23,000 acres. Some of the large plantations have been broken up into small farms, because of depression, the owners finding farming unprofitable.

The sufferings from tenancy are numerous. The children of tenants are denied an education, forced to spend the majority of their time in the field. The tenants cannot establish an independent life, but are dependent almost entirely upon the planter for every breath they draw. In a few cases some tenants, who have the right to bargain off their crops, have a slightly higher standard of living. They are not dependent upon the landlord to furnish all the food, clothing, and supplies. But the high rentals nearly reduce this group to the same level of the standing renters and croppers.

Tenancy provides the system of robbery by the white ruling class of the Negro victims. From the plantation lord down to the petty merchant, each has a hand in exploiting and robbing these people. The creditor always collects his debt, owed by the tenant, from the landlord, who in turn sufficiently increases the amount to reimburse him against any loss he may sustain in undertaking such a risk.

Peonage

Tenancy has an accompanying evil known as peonage. Peonage is the scourge that enslaves thousands of black agrarian workers. To prevent any possible chance of the tenants leaving the lands or shifting from one plantation to another, the system of peonage has been adopted. *Peonage is the sharpest expression of a present-day feudal social antagonism (slavery remnant) which firmly fastens the chains of bondage upon its hapless victims, to assure the plantation owners of permanent, cheap, and docile labor, thereby securing the position of these parasites to continue their oppression and exploitation and drive to the bottomless economic abyss this "caste of untouchables."*

Enforcing Peonage

After the Civil War, the Southern States were intent to secure free labor. Many enacted vagrancy laws which compelled every free person to enter the service of some planter and remain there regardless of wages received. The amount of wages was determined by the former masters. One found without a job was arrested and convicted, and either placed on the chain gang to build public highways or leased to landlords. This in reality was a return to slavery. The Washington government interrupted this practice. But, after the withdrawal of troops from the conquered area, the Negroes were disfranchised and the democratic rights previously granted were ignored. Various states, upheld by the courts, passed elusive laws providing for involuntary servitude for debt. States adopting this system were Florida, Georgia, Alabama, North and South Carolina, and Mississippi. Failure to obey contracts for employment, the slightest violation of a contract, or temporary unemployment, drew the wrath of this law which was enforced by the rural courts. A few states attempted to hide the actual enslavement of Negroes with "hidden" plantations on which men, women, and children were kept in involuntary servitude, peonage.

To hold a tenant by fair or foul methods became the cardinal ambition of the planter. To lose his laborer meant to lose his profits. The crops would not be planted, consequently, no harvesting.

A State Law on Peonage

The case of *Bailey v. the State of Alabama* upheld a law which provided that any person who made a contract in writing to perform a service for another and thereby obtained money or other personal property from such person with attempt to defraud the person, and who left his services without performing that service or refunding the money or property, was guilty of a misdemeanor. The law further provided that any person who made a contract in writing for the rent of land, and obtained money or personal property from the landlord with the intention of deceiving him and left without performing such service, refunding the money, or paying for the property, was also guilty of a misdemeanor. The penalty for the offence was a fine not exceeding $300 and, in default of payment, imprisonment for a period of not more than 12 months. To make this law further effective it was amended so as to make the failure of any person who entered such a contract to perform the service or cultivate the land or refund the money or restore the goods, prima facie evidence of intent to injure or defraud his landlord. According to the decision delivered by the Alabama Supreme Court, the accused should not be allowed to testify as to his intent or purpose, or "to rebut a statutory presumption." Inasmuch as employers thereafter made such contracts with their laborers when only the employer and employee were present, it became an easy matter to enforce compliance with such contracts through minor rural courts.

Repressive Measures

A way of securing peons is for an employer or his agent to go to a town or city and hire a group of laborers. He agrees to pay certain wages and transportation and provide the necessary provisions from the commissary, the company store. The laborers, indebted to their employed, trade out their meager wages at the company store. By false methods, trickery, and even foul play the employer keeps the peon in perpetual debt. What books are kept (by the planter only) have false entries. A peon with a large family is most desirable to the planter, who afforded a greater opportunity to increase his robbery of large numbers of permanent victims through his false book-keeping system. Oft-times to assure that the peons do not attempt to run away, their children are taken from them.

To keep the peons on the plantations it is necessary to establish iron authority over them. The overseer is the terrorist of every plantation. He uses the whip and gun to strike terror among the peons, subjecting them to the will of the boss and slavery conditions. Women and children alike become the personal property of the white master. The latter grow up in ignorance, and the former are prostituted by the many white masters. By the use of sheer force these people are not allowed to leave the plantation, only on very rare occasions. If perchance a victim escapes, he is arrested under false pre-texts, as jumping a contract, cheating, or false promises. Generally there is not a trial. But the officer returns the unfortunate peon to the plantation camp, where he is severely punished.

Convict Labor

Convict labor and the chain gang have resulted from peonage. The need of the South for a large supply of laborers has been used as a pretext for the landlords to conscript men and women. A flimsy charge would place one in jail. Planters bargained with the courts for their prisoners, paying the fines, and putting many in involuntary servitude. By forced restraint and co-operation from constables, sheriffs, and other court officials, the prisoners released by the courts to the planters are kept in bondage and avenues of escape are closed. If one gets away, bloodhounds are put on his trail and when caught he is subjected to fiendish torture. Planters when brought before the courts on charges of peonage and using convict labor have answered that they had to whip Negroes brutally once in a while to keep them from rebel-ling.

In 1919 in Elaine, Arkansas, a rebellion of Negroes in peonage took place. These victims, because of the worst forms of oppression, struck a blow for economic liberty. But they were shot down, overpowered, and arrested. A mob court held a mock trial and sentenced 67 to long prison terms and 12 to death.

During the Mississippi flood it was revealed that peonage was rampant. The planter objected to having their peons go to the Red Cross camps for fear of escape. They did not consent until they received assurance from the Red Cross officials that their "niggers" would be returned to them.

The state, using the national guard, compelled the peons to work throughout the flooded area. The most brutal methods were employed to prevent all attempts to escape. However, many fled to the North, telling of the horrible conditions existing on the peonage farms. This was in 1928.

The fact that there exist on the statute books of the federal government laws prohibiting peonage does not safeguard the rights of Negroes. This remnant of slavery, fastening its iron hold upon millions of unfortunate victims, has its roots in a scoundrelly social order whose dastardly rulers in their mad rush to amass riches out of the sweat and blood of the workers and peasants exploit and oppress the entire toiling class. The defenseless Negroes, considered as a caste of "untouchables," and who in the majority are agrarian workers, have not been liberated. Amendments to the present constitution will not free them. Only an agrarian revolution, with the proletariat assuming the hegemony under the leadership of Communists, will finally achieve freedom for this oppressed potential nation.

"It is a Yankee bourgeois lie to say that the yoke of slavery has been lifted in the United States."*

These social antagonisms (remnants of slavery) "stink of the disgusting atmosphere of the old slave market. This is downright robbery and slave-whipping barbarism at the peak of capitalist 'culture'."*

*Resolution of the Communist International on the *Negro Questions in the United States*.

For a Strict Leninist Analysis of the Negro National Question in the United States
[*The Communist*, October 1932]

"The American Negro," by J. S. Allen, a pamphlet dealing with the Negro question in the U.S.A., contains some very excellent factual material. This material exposes the present position of the 12,000,000 Negroes in this country in a glaring manner. It gives the economic and the political status of the oppressed nation which is the social outcast of "American Nordic Society."

The base for the terrific exploitation and oppression of the Negro masses is a social and economic one. Over 9,000,000 Negroes live in the South, and the majority of this number inhabit the Black Belt. The Black Belt is a continuous stretch of territory which (according to the author) runs through eleven states. In this territory the Negroes are the majority of the population and are mainly tenant farmers and peons. They are deprived of their elemental democratic rights, all power resting in the hands of the white ruling class minority. Repressive measures of slavery days are employed to keep the Negro masses in subjection to strengthen the economic and political position of the white ruling class.

The Negro worker in the North is shown as an integral part of the working class in practically all of the basic industries. Unemployment has hit this worker hardest during the present economic crisis.

Discrimination and Jim-Crowism are wide-spread. The American Federation of Labor is an outstanding example of carrying through this policy. An interesting section is devoted to the Jim-Crow practices in the army which have been carried to the extent of disarming and disbanding several Negro regiments.

Statistical data is given on lynchings and legal frame-ups covering a period of years and is quite inclusive, giving the economic and social cause for this American pastime.

The pamphlet exposes the misleaders of the labor movement and those among the Negro masses who are great hindrances to the revolutionizing of the struggle for Negro rights. It is pointed out that class solidarity, a fighting alliance of black and white workers in the struggle, is of utmost importance to the building up of the national liberation movement, as part and parcel of the struggle of the working class to overthrow capitalism.

The accompanying map of the Black Belt strikingly shows the old slave South, in which territory the national oppression of the Negro, remnants of slavery, takes its most acute form. Here the plantation system and all its accompanying evils (peonage, share cropping, debt slavery, etc.) persists up to the present day in all their most brutal forms. Here is where the national oppression against the Negro nation is sharpest. It shows where basic organizational work must be carried on to win the Negroes to struggle, together with other workers, in the liberation movement and for emancipation.

The material arms one with undeniable facts which substantiate the Communist program of liberation. These basic facts are useful for agitators and provide a firm foundation for our theoretical line.

After pointing out the enslavement of the Negro masses, their superexploitation and terrific persecution, the Communist program of struggle for Negro rights and complete emancipation is given.

However, in dealing with this all-important and complicated national question in the United States, formulations are made which reveal unclarity and in their sum total, amount to a concession to bourgeois liberalism. These inexact formulations are a distortion of Leninist theory on the national questions. Chief among these errors are the following:

1. That the Negroes suffer from a *"special caste system and brutal persecution based on the color line."*
2. That "the right of self-determination is *a part of* the general struggle for Negro rights," (My emphasis—B. D. A.)
3. That self-determination means the right for the Negroes "to rule *themselves* within their own state boundaries." (My emphasis—B. D. A.)

The first formulation conveys the impression that Jim-Crowism and national oppression of the Negroes has its origin in the differences between races, and as such rejects the Leninist conception of the Negro question as a *national question*. It is clearly a concession to the current bourgeois racial theories.

In order to justify the ruthless oppression of the Negro masses, the white bourgeois ideologists build up false race theories. These are designed to prove the inherent inferiority of the Negro peoples. In these theories racial differences, that is differences in the color of skin, texture of hair, etc., between the Negro and white peoples—purely physical and extra-historical factors—become an explanation and justification of national oppression.

The real economic and social essence of the Negro question in the United States consists not in racial differences, but in the differences between economic and cultural developments of Negro and white peoples under conditions of a capitalist social order. The idea of race superiority and inferiority has its roots in and expresses the economic class relations of slave and slave owners, whether it be chattel or wage slavery.

Consequently, the color of one's skin is used to designate one's position in the realm of human society. In this instance the white skin is made to typify the peak of "capitalist culture," the zenith of "capitalist civilization," and the last word in science and intellectuality. On the other hand, the black skin is made to symbolize "low culture," "barbarity," "born rapists" and "incapability."

The white ruling class, therefore, by causing such false theories to spread and take root, is able to cover up its own real class position and its national oppression of the Negro masses. The difference between the whites and the Negroes, the color of skin and the texture of hair, a physical difference, is used by the white ruling class as an instrument for the more intense exploitation and oppression of the Negro masses.

The classification of peoples into color and race types is purely artificial, but is seized upon by the bourgeois ideologists as the decisive link to strengthen their myth of "white Nordic supremacy and Negro inferiority."

The Negro bourgeoisie dominated by the white capitalists and imperialists give support to these false slave theories. This creates still another condition for the continued special exploitation of the Negroes on the land and in industries. The segregated Negro areas in metropolitan cities (Harlem, Southside Chicago, etc.) give expression to the vicious imperialist ideology—keep the Negro "in his place." These districts are supported by the Negro politicians and reformists leaders, because of the privileged class position it gives them for betraying the liberation struggle of the Negro people, and at the same time help maintain the division of Negro and white workers. In this manner color ideologies play an important role in sharpening the oppression of the Negro masses and in keeping the Negro and white workers separated.

A social and political super-structure which consists of the denial of democratic rights to the Negro population, full equalities, and the right of self-determination, and the whole system of Jim-Crowism and segregation is built upon the social and economic position of the Negroes.

To maintain that the Negro question is a "race question," or that the oppression of Negroes is based upon the "color line" is to blur over its social and economic essence; in other words, to capitulate to bourgeois race theories. Such a conception is equivalent to a deep underestimation of the revolutionary content of the struggles of the Negro masses for national liberation. Objectively, failure to see the powerful social and economic factors underlying the national liberation struggle of the Negro people, reduces the movement to a feeble opposition against American imperialism.

The second error, the formulation that "the right of self-determination" is "*a part of* the general struggle for Negro rights," is an incorrect formulation. The last resolution on the Negro question in the U.S., clearly states,

> "The struggle of the Communists for the equal rights of the Negroes applies to all Negroes, in the North as well as in the South. The struggle for this slogan embraces all or almost all of the important special interests of the Negroes in the North, but not in the South, where the main Communist slogan must be: *The right of self-determination of the Negroes in the Black Belt.* These two slogans, however, are most closely connected. The Negroes in the North are very much interested in winning the right of self-determination of the Negro population of the Black Belt and can thereby hope for strong support for the establishment of true equality of the Negroes in the North. In the South the Negroes are suffering no less but still more than in the North from the glaring lack of equality; for the most part the struggle for their most urgent partial demands in the Black Belt is nothing more than the struggle for their equal rights, and only the fulfillment of their main slogans, the right of self-determination in the Black Belt, can assure them of true equality."

To place the right of self-determination as "*a part of*" the general struggle for Negro rights is to blur over the main struggle in the Black Belt. The *concrete* requirements of the liberation struggles of the Negroes are not simply the struggle for equal rights, but the right of self-determination of the Negroes of the Black Belt, which cannot be realized without the fulfillment of the two *basic demands*, confiscation of the land and state unity of the Black Belt. In the North the main slogan is equal rights, but in the South it is the right of self-determination. Social equality in the South can only be realized by the Negro population through the right of self-determination.

The important special interests of the Negroes in the North, i.e., the right to have jobs that only whites are given; the right to live wherever they choose, (not in segregated areas), equal pay for equal work; breaking down discrimination and Jim-Crowism in practice, in fact the right to enjoy the present rights given the white workers, plus the rights which can be won by the white and Negro workers, are the democratic rights which must be granted. At the same time the guarantee for equal rights of the Negro in the North will be secured by the winning of the right of self-determination in the Black Belt. Therefore, the Negroes of the South can expect a strong ally in the Northern Negro industrial proletariat, who will give support to the struggles of the Negroes in the Black Belt for the right of self-determination.

In the South the above democratic rights are denied the Negroes. But in addition there is in the Black Belt a complete denial of every elementary right, *i.e.*, the right to vote; right to equal educational facilities; the right to hold governmental office; right to organize, free speech, in most reactionary parts of the Black Belt. All governmental, legislative and judicial authority is concentrated in the hands of the white minority, bourgeoisie and landlords. "*Therefore, the overthrow of this class rule* in the Black Belt is unconditionally necessary in the struggle for the Negroes' right to self-determination." (C.I. Resolution.)

The fulfillment of this demand means at the same time to overthrow the yoke of American imperialism.

To carelessly lump together these demands—"equal rights" and "right of self-determination"—is identical to the attitude of the socialists and white liberals who give lip-service to the slogan of equal rights for the Negroes.

Right to self-determination *raises the question of power* for the Negro population in the Black Belt. It means wrestling the power from the white minority exploiters. This direct question of power is the guarantee to secure equal rights for the Negro population in the South. It is a *basic, fundamental* demand of the liberation struggle of the Negroes in the Black Belt. This slogan ". . . *once thoroughly understood by the Negro masses and adopted as their slogan . . . will lead them into the struggle for the overthrow of the power of the ruling bourgeoisie. . .*" (C. I. Resolution.) The slogan of the right of self-determination is therefore a slogan of national rebellion.

The third error, the right of the Negro majority in the Black Belt, "*to rule themselves* within their own state boundaries. . ." is a confused formulation. The C. I. resolution very clearly and decisively explains the incorrectness of such a formulation.

"Every plan regarding the establishment of the Negro state with an exclusively Negro population in America (and of course, still more exporting it
to Africa) is nothing but an unreal and reactionary caricature of the fulfillment of the right of self-determination of the Negroes, and every attempt to isolate and transport the Negroes would have the most damaging
effect upon their interest; above all it would violate the right of the Negro
farmers in the Black Belt not only to their present residences and their
land, but also to the land owned by the white landlords and cultivated by
Negro labor." Again we quote the CI resolution, "It would not be right of
self-determination only in cases which concerned *exclusively* the Negroes.
. . ."

"To rule themselves" means that the Negro majority in the Black Belt
should have the right to govern *only the Negroes*, in such areas where there
is are all-black populations, and not the white minority, which lives in the
continuous stretch of territory where the majority of the population are Negroes, constituting the Black Belt. Furthermore the white minority, the present oppressors, who have all power in their hands, would not, according to
Comrade Allen's incorrect formulation, be subjected to this rule. They would
maintain their own small states which would constantly be a menace to the
Negro republics.

The slavery system and national oppression of the Negroes in the South
has its root in the large landed estates of the white exploiters. Without the
expropriation of these landlords there can not be any taking over of power.
Without an agrarian revolution there can be no true right to self-
determination. To leave the large landed properties in possession of the
white landlords would continue the present day slavery and robbery of millions of Negroes.

There is little difference in this wrong formulation and the non-
revolutionary Garvey theory of "Africa for the Africans." This theory supports the imperialists in their attempt to separate the Negro masses from the
white revolutionary workers. It weakens the struggle against the imperialist
oppressors.

The theoretical defenders of white chauvinism would gladly accept this
formula "*to rule themselves*," and give the Negroes a state for themselves,
where they would have no governmental, judicial, and legislative authority
over the small white population.

To accept the formulation "to rule *themselves* within their own state
boundaries" would not only be a concession to reactionary Negro bourgeois
nationalism (Garvey) but to white chauvinism as well.

The above mistakes in formulations dealing with the national question
and the right to self-determination of the Negroes in the Black Belt distort
the Marxian-Leninist line. They are inexact and inaccurate. They are confus-
ing and hinder the hastening of real clarity on the program of the Communist
Party U.S.A., for the national liberation of the Negro population.

CHAPTER 4
SCOTTSBORO DOCUMENTS

Document 1
Fond 515, Files of the Communist Party of the United States in the
Comintern Archives.

> Telegram from the Executive Committee
> League of Struggle for Negro Rights to Governor of Alabama, April 9,
> 1931.
> The League of Struggle for Negro Rights vigorously protests the de-
> liberate frame-up against the nine Negro youths and their railroading to
> the electric chair. This organization of ten thousand membership de-
> mands that you stop this legal lynching and holds you responsible to stay
> the hands of the lynch mob.
> EXECUTIVE COMMITTEE
> LEAGUE OF STRUGGLE FOR NEGRO RIGHTS
> B.D. AMIS, President.

Document 2
Fond 515, Files of the Communist Party of the United States in the
Comintern Archives.

> Statement by the Central Committee, Communist Party USA, April 9,
> 1931.
> The Communist Party of the United States calls upon the white
> workers of Alabama, the white workers of the whole south and the whole
> United States to make the cause of the Negro workers their own cause.
> We call upon both Negro and white workers to unite and to rally to the
> cause of these 9 Negro boys who are being lynched in Scottsboro.
> The Communist Party calls upon all working class and Negro organi-
> zations to adopt strong resolutions of protest, and to wire these to the
> governor of Alabama and to the *Daily Worker*. But wires to such capital-
> ist officials alone will do no good, you must organize at the greatest pos-
> sible speed mass meetings and militant mass demonstrations against this
> crime. Let the southern ruling class know that the working class will not
> tolerate further continuance of their bloody crimes against our class!

Certain "reformist" organizations, claiming to represent the interest of the Negroes, such as the National Association for the Advancement of Colored People, the Universal Negro Improvement Association, the Urban League, etc., are, in fact, under the leadership and control of middle class reformists who, we are perfectly aware, cannot be depended upon to rally those organizations in defense of these helpless boys of Scottsboro. These reformist leaders can be expected, as usual, only to betray the Negro masses, and in this case it is easy to betray by pretending to believe that these boys are getting a "legal trial," whereas these reformists claim only to be "against illegal lynching." The Communist Party calls upon the rank and file members of these organizations nevertheless to give their support to the campaign to save these defenseless Negro boys.

We demand a united front of all working and farming masses of this country to stop the legal lynching at Scottsboro.

Workers, black and white—organize monster mass meetings, militant demonstrations! Let the southern ruling class know that we will tolerate their crimes against our class and the persecuted Negro race no longer!

The death penalty for lynchers! Stop the legal lynching at Scottsboro!

Document 3
Fond 515, Files of the Communist Party of the United States in the Comintern Archives.

NEGRO DEPARTMENT C.C.
P.O. Box 87, Station D.
New York, N.Y.

April 9, 1931

Dear Comrades:

The Central Committee instructs you to immediately arrange a series of mass protest meetings against the legal lynching of the 9 Negro youths in Scottsboro, Alabama.

The District Committee is responsible to initiate this campaign. These meetings must be held in every section of the districts. Large mass meetings of Negro and white workers, native and foreign-born, must be mobilized for active participation in raising a huge protest against the ruling landlords and capitalists and their court, linking up this specific case with our preparations for May Day.

Lynchings must be a central figure in the May Day demonstrations. The local persecutions of Negro and white workers must likewise be closely connected with this latest outburst of terrorism.

The steps to be taken in this campaign are as follows:

1. The Party organizations to initiate the campaign.
2. The L.S.N.R. to make official calls for united fronts to all mass organizations, Negro organizations, clubs, fraternal orders, etc.
3. The YCL must likewise issue a call to all youth and sport clubs.

4. Each organization to hold protest meetings adopting protest resolutions and to send telegrams of protest to Governor Miller of Alabama.
5. The legal lynching of these 9 Negro youths must be a central figure in our preparations for May First.
6. Organizational gains must be achieved to build the *Liberator* and the L.S.N.R.

Immediate response must be made as to what steps you are taking to carry through these instructions. When all arrangements are under way, report fully what they are.

Resolutions of meetings must immediately, at the conclusion of the demonstrations, be communicated to the Central Office and the *Daily Worker*.

All organizations, especially Negro organizations, must be visited and their sentiment aroused against this terror. Each must be stirred up and urged to hold protest meetings and send protest resolutions and telegrams to the state government.

You are to make the mass character of the demonstration the center of your reliance. These must be conducted with a view to continuing the movement and repeating the demonstrations on a mounting scale of mass participation.

Comradely your.

B.D. Amis [FOR THE CENTRAL COMMITTEE]

Document 4
Fond 515, Files of the Communist Party of the United States in the Comintern Archives.

THE LIBERATOR [New York City]   April 21, 1931
Dear Editor:

We write to you most urgently to draw your attention to the necessity of using the full power of the Negro press to defeat one of the worst crimes against our people that has ever been produced in the backward regions of the South. You are doubtless aware that at Scottsboro, Alabama, 9 Negro boys, ranging from 14 to 20 years of age, have recently been jammed through a hasty mock trial in a courthouse surrounded by a mob of ten thousand howling whites, and 8 of them were tried and sentenced to death in the electric chair within a space of four days.

In my joint capacity as editor of the *Liberator* and an official of the League of Struggle for Negro Rights, I have been working hard to get at the facts, have been in touch with other organizations and leaders, and, together with these, have succeeded in getting two attorneys from New York to go down to Birmingham, Alabama, where these lawyers have gotten into the jail and have seen the 8 boys who are sentenced to death. The facts we learned from them are in main points that follow:

1. They are typical honest and innocent hardworking lads of tender age and absolutely not of the hardened sort that could possibly be conceived to have committed the crime of violent attack upon women.

2. These boys, who are too simple and direct, as well as too young to be able to dissimulate under the pressure of a case of this kind, have told our attorneys a perfectly straightforward story accounting for their moves and everything that could possibly bear upon the case, and our attorneys assure us that there is not the slightest doubt that the boys are telling the truth—that they had absolutely nothing to do with the affair and had never been near the women at all.

3. Their so-called "trial" was nothing less than the first act of a lynching, jammed through in almost the same number of hours that it would have required to perform the usual style of lynching under a tree in the open. They had no defense whatever that is worthy of mention.

4. Their so-called attorneys, according to our best information, were appointed by the court after the attorneys had openly expressed their desire to see the boys executed.

5. Everyone concerned in the case sneeringly regarded it as only a variation of the ordinary lynching; it being openly told to the howling mob outside that they could be assured it was unnecessary for them to hang the boys because the trial would be "almost as quick, and with the same results."

6. The boys (8 of them) stand condemned to die on July 10th. The 9th boy is being held back on some technical grounds for another trial.

7. The attorneys who were engaged by the International Labor Defense, New York City, in cooperation with us, have taken the first steps for an appeal, and from every legal aspect they would have every reason to expect success if it were possible for a colored man or even 9 colored children to receive a square deal from the "white supremacy" courts of Alabama.

8. However, the whole case shows itself to be a question of mass pressure. The background of the case is a terrible economic situation in that section of Alabama, where the colored farmers (share-croppers and tenants), and the white share-croppers and tenant farmers of the same class, have been having a great deal of friction with the white landlords. There is quite a movement against the usual gouging of the tenants and even a certain tendency for the white tenants and the Negro tenants to make common cause against the landlords.

You will doubtless have noticed as well that the Southern white ruling class newspapers have recently been trying to stir up every possible hysteria against the race, doubtless being influenced more or less by the desire to start the fight between whites and blacks of the same class in order to divert the pressure from this case. The great unemployment of that section has added to the electricity in the air, especially as starving unemployed workers, black and white are actually organizing unemployed councils together, with no color line. Only a few days ago, for instance, the Ku Klux Klan attempted to break up by violence an unemployed council of Negroes and Whites at Greenville, S.C., where conditions are much the same.

It is my belief that the horrible tragedy which is now about to take place in the death of these boys on July 10th is a challenge which every Negro in America and the whole world must take up and fight out to the last ditch. I believe that if we can save these boys, this one act alone will give new courage to our people and will help immensely to turn the tide against the lynching of our people.

But as I said, it is a question of mass pressure. I am one of those who believes that we ourselves can exercise mass pressure in a case so horrible as the present one. It would be impossible to imagine a case where there is so much reason to fight.

Will the Negro press arise to this occasion and fight as one man to save those innocent boys?

I must urgently request you to throw your paper into this fight to save these boys. I believe the facts are before you. We have received rather extensive stories from the Crusader News Service to which I believe you also subscribe. Also, the *Liberator* will gladly cooperate in any way requested.

But I urge you to be quick about it! It takes time to get a real mass movement under way. We have already had conferences with various organizations, including Communists, trade unions, working men's clubs, etc., and others, and it has already been arranged that a demonstration on a large scale will take place on the first day of May in every city in the United States. Arrangements are being made to hold these demonstrations in the Southern cities as well as the Northern, such as Birmingham, Atlanta, Tampa, New Orleans, Chattanooga, and San Antonio. Our belief is that it is necessary to get thousands of our people into these demonstrations with banners inscribed with the demand to stop the legal lynching of these Negro boys at Scottsboro.

We most earnestly hope that you will respond to this request.

Sincerely yours,

B.D. Amis

EDITOR, THE *LIBERATOR*

Document 5
"Croppers in Southern United States Fight to Live"
By B. D. Amis
International Press Correspondence, August 20, 1931.

In the southern states of Tennessee, Georgia, Alabama and North and South Carolina, large sections of the Negro people and portions of the advanced white workers are thoroughly aroused over the hideous and farcical condemnation of the nine youths and the imprisonment of over 36 Camp Hill peasants. These same people welcome the mass campaign of the Communist Party, of the League of Struggle for Negro Rights, and of the International Labor Defense as the only **genuine** method that will force the Alabama ruling class and its courts to release their deadly clutch and give freedom to these working class youths and croppers.

The Negro masses, bound by the ponderous chains of American imperialism, doubly exploited and oppressed by the large plantation bosses and owners of finance capital, have but one way out—to organize and fight.

Recently in Alabama, in the heart of the Black Belt, the lowest category of farm laborers, and the most oppressed of the Negro masses (those who today are in slavery, in the true sense of the word), the croppers, have struck a blow for freedom against the plantation bosses.

The first of July found the plantation bosses cutting off entirely the croppers from their food provisions. After planting and cultivating the crops there is a lag in the season of from one to two months, during which period the cropper is turned loose to starve or get along as best he can. The monthly 24-pound sack of flour is cut off from the families and all other provisions, food and clothing, are denied them.

A few months back the Alabama legislature was startled to learn that the croppers and tenant farmers in certain counties of the state were reading radical literature and talking of organizing into a Croppers Union. This immediately caused the legislature to work for the enactment of a law that would bring severe punishment to those who wrote such literature and also to those who dared to distribute the same among their "peaceful niggers," and "incite them to riot." All literature was confiscated and the croppers threatened with beatings, lynchings, and being driven off the plantations.

But this attempt to terrorize the croppers and to crush their organization did not have the effect that was intended. The call to organize a Croppers Union was answered by a tremendous response from all the Negro croppers in this territory, and even included a few white croppers. There was a conscious desire of the croppers to build the organization, with the perspective of creating a struggle during the slack periods, and to present demands to the plantation bosses for a continuance of their sparse rations and a fight for their very lives.

*

The stubborn spirit of resistance, the firm determination to break the yoke of the oppressors, was sharply revealed when the brutal lackeys of the plantation bosses swooped down upon a meeting of the Croppers Union.

In the clash which followed one cropper, Ralph Gray, was mortally wounded, but not before the croppers had wounded Sheriff Young and some of his deputized thugs. The white terrorists got in action. Scores of croppers and tenant farmers were herded into the Dadeville jail; beatings, threats of violence and third degree methods were used upon the prisoners to cause them to reveal the identity of the organizers of the union. But these methods have been unsuccessful, the croppers remaining firm and steadfast.

The second attack took place the following evening upon the home of Gray. The sadistic deputies and mob terrorists riddled the body of Gray, who was in bed wounded with bullets. They clubbed the baby children over the heads with the butts of their guns, and lashed the women as they hurled at them threatening words of rape and lynching. Gray was thrown into a car where he died, supposedly on his way to the hospital. The other members of the family were driven from the house, which was set on fire.

The sheriff and his mob evidently murdered other croppers. When asked the whereabouts of those who were missing, this butcher of the southern plantation bosses answered, "they've gone to cut stove-wood," which is the local way of saying that they were dead.

The meeting of the croppers union, held to discuss the question of struggle against starvation and to protest against the attempted legal lynching of the Scottsboro boys, proves to the American oppressors of the Negro masses that there is a rising tide of discontent among these workers and they will no longer permit black men and women and children to be ground down under the iron and bloody heal of the Southern big landlords and capitalists. Neither will they permit the attempt to burn in the electric chair eight innocent Negro boys, without raising a stormy protest.

The latest attempt of the Alabama big bosses and plantation owners to crush the Croppers' Union and to strike terror into the hearts of the Negro masses, is being answered by the international working class.

The Negro masses, together with the advanced section of the white workers, must continue to build a powerful mass defense movement to stop the terrorization of the Negroes in the Camp Hill section of Alabama and build a broad defense campaign as in the Scottsboro case, which will be the only movement that will save the lives and liberties of these croppers and tenant farmers who are now languishing in the Dadeville jail.

Document 6
Fond 515, Files of the Communist Party of the United States in the Comintern Archives.

Negro Bureau of the Comintern
B.D. Amis Speech at the XIII Plenum, CPUSA, 1931.

In the 20 minutes I have I want to deal with one point. And that is because the Party today is engaged in such a struggle that it is necessary that we must have the fullest clarification relative to the struggles we are conducting for Negro rights in order that this tremendous influence we have among the Negro masses may be turned into organizational results. No one will deny the fact that the Party has an overwhelming amount of influence among the Negro masses. This is best shown in their participation in the various demonstrations that the Party, the TUUL have held, also in the hunger marches and in the numerous other campaigns the Party has conducted. On August 1st, in the Party demonstrations against the war danger, here we can see a great upward trend in the number of participants of Negroes in the hundreds of demonstrations. For instance, in places like in the North, in Minnesota, etc., we see that these workers are not so very familiar with our systematic and energetic fight against the war danger, for the protection of the Soviet Union, but because of the correct approach of the Party, we were able to draw out large numbers to demonstrate. This influence the Party has, has been the result of the Party beginning to conduct gigantic struggles in the fight for Negro rights. We have recorded positive achievements since the last Plenum. For instance, the Yokinen trial in New York which laid the very foundation for the absolute turn in our work in the Negro field.

The next large struggle was the developing of a large mass movement around the Scottsboro campaign and here, comrades, I want to dwell for quite a few moments, for the reason that in the Scottsboro campaign we have for the first time in the Party a gigantic struggle which has two aspects in the struggle for Negro rights, the national questions and the class question.

Because of the united front policy we have carried on, we were able to mobilize hundreds of thousands of Negroes to participate in the building up of a mass defense movement in the Scottsboro campaign. However, because of the fact that we were able to win the mothers of all the boys to support us in this campaign, because we were able to mobilize thousands of Negro workers to help us build up this movement, we did not exploit these opportunities to the fullest extent.

The comrades did not understand the peculiar role of the Negro workers. For instance, when we decided to bring every mother to the North to conduct an energetic campaign in order to mobilize thousands of Negro workers to protest against the frame-up, the comrades were not conscious of the necessity to pay special attention to the care of these mothers. I want to state that I believe that our comrades in Philadelphia do not receive our CC directives or they don't read them. We were very careful when we knew we had in our hands a weapon which could become the sharpest instrument with which we could break down the illusions of the white liberals and petty-bourgeois reformist Negroes by utilizing these mothers to help build up this mass movement. In every district, however, we see a looseness and a most criminal carelessness in the handling of the mothers.

In Philadelphia, we sent Mrs. Powell, the mother of the one of the boys. What did they do? We stated in our directive that these mothers must be placed with responsible Party comrades who should have the task of always and constantly guiding and watching over them. Mrs. Powell, however, was placed with the rankest sort of white chauvinist who put her to work washing dishes, scrubbing floors, washing dyties, etc.

Now, comrades, however, after the Philadelphia comrades had this deplorable situation drawn to their attention, some steps were made to correct this. But after Mrs. Powell was brought here to New York, where we take pride in having certain facilities to make these mothers more comfortable and help develop them, even here our comrades fell down on the job, placing her in an isolated home or rather a meeting hall in the most foul air and dirty quarters.

This shows what, comrades? First of all, that the comrades were not aware of the hazardous situation they placed us in. If our enemies would have found out that we handled the mothers like we did, what would have been the result? Take it the other way. If we knew these mothers were handled like this by the NAACP, would we not jump at their throats in meetings, conferences, etc.? Our comrades do not recognize that in dealing with the question, we have a special question and we cannot treat this question like we treat the ordinary question and like we treat the white workers. From now on, the comrades must recognize that fact that in dealing with the Negro question they have a special task. And that is our task to show the Negro workers—yes, we are going to fight for their rights and to show them we are going to carry on an energetic campaign in order to prove that the things we put in writing will be carried out in practice. In the Camp Hill case, it was a result of our Scottsboro campaign, that the Negro peasants in Alabama were willing to carry on a campaign linking this case up with the Scottsboro case and other campaigns we were carrying on.

We noticed a decided lagging in this campaign. However, there was another campaign which proved a sort of a boomerang. The Chicago massacre and here we find a rise in the curve. The struggles that the comrades in Chicago conducted gave a little bit more of an impetus to the Scottsboro and the Camp Hill campaign.

Now as to some of the mistakes of the Scottsboro campaign. First I think we have to charge ourselves with making these mistakes and one of the crassest in my opinion in this campaign was when we started out to build block and neighborhood committees. Not that we should not have built them. This is the most effective way in which we could reach the masses by our united front from below, but we began to build block committees and neighborhood committees in certain districts and restricted and narrowed the base only to the issue of struggle to save the nine boys. This is not the correct policy. The policy should have been, and we did change afterwards, that the workers drawn into the block and neighborhood committees should not only be drawn into the struggle to save the nine Scottsboro boys but that we should raise the level of their struggles, draw them into further political campaigns that we would develop their class-consciousness and develop their mood for struggle against all forms of oppression and exploitation.

Another mistake and this was noticeable in almost every district. The comrades in trying to build united front movements from below followed in the tail of the Negro misleaders such [the] NAACP and churches, going there and appealing to the "fair-play" of these misleaders and for them to appeal to "their" masses in the campaign. We would have built up a more genuine mass movement if we had absolutely ignored these misleaders and went about building the block and neighborhood committees and we would have drawn thousands more into the struggle than we did. Another mistake was the open arms with which we accepted one of the worst types of reactionary misleaders of the Negro masses, when Pickens wrote the International Labor Defense and sent them a few dollars endorsing the campaign, we came out with great big headlines welcoming Pickens into the struggle, stating that he had joined the struggle without exposing his reactionary role and without telling the masses that his action was caused not by his sincerity but by the mass pressure forcing him to take such a step. This we failed to do and this is a bad mistake. Closely connected with this was another serious mistake which I made myself and I want to take full responsibility for this. And this is the editorial which appeared in the *Liberator* last week where we also gave the crassest manifestation of Right wing opportunism in appealing to the bourgeois press to more energetically take up the struggle for Negro rights. I will not go into the details of what was the content of the editorial but it is sufficient to state that the contents were of such character that there was a tendency to create false illusions among the Negro masses that they could rely on their Negro reformist leaders, that they would begin to struggle for their rights. Also that we somehow expected these petty-bourgeois reactionary newspaper leaders to use the columns of their press to expose the white terror and oppression and exploitation of the Negro masses. Another danger is that we did not link up the struggle of the Negro masses with the struggle of the white workers. And this brought into more sharp expression that in this appeal we absolutely distorted the role of the *Liberator*. And after we get through reading this editorial one would think that the Negro press will become an effective force to mobilize the Negro masses for struggle. Then there is no room for the *Liberator*?

Such mistakes hinder and hamper our struggle in mobilizing masses of Negro workers to participate in joint struggle with the white workers and it is necessary at this time that whatever we put into the press, our policies, must be clear-out decisive and correct.

Now comrades, in regard to the struggle today in the Negro field, some comrades have raised the question, because of these partial successes (and I want to state that in Chicago where they have had partial success that they are now on the brink of the danger point). Here is a tremendous amount of influence built up among the Negro workers in the South side of Chicago and now we have an opportunity to show that we as a Communist Party, as a Bolshevik Party, can take this influence among the thousands of Negro workers and turn it into organizational gains and build our Party, that we can build our revolutionary unions, that we can build our LSNR, that we can build our *Liberator* into a mass organ. Unless we are able to realize some organizational results from this mass influence that we have in Chicago we will have to acknowledge that we are absolutely very weak, and the campaign will almost amount to naught. Some of the comrades realize the successes of these struggles of the share croppers in Alabama, because of the struggles in Chicago and Scottsboro, because of the militancy of the Negro workers in Birmingham in fighting police terror the comrades say they think it is time to raise a new perspective—whether we are in an insurrectionary period or not. We must have a new perspective.

We are not ready now to raise the question of a new perspective, neither are the Negro masses in a period of insurrection. Our task is to develop further the struggles of the Negro workers, economic struggles, political struggles, struggles for their day to day needs. Another task is to link up the struggles of the Negro masses with the struggles of the white proletariat. If we concern ourselves with these major tasks and develop the fighting political consciousness the next stage of their struggles will come and we will not have to worry about looking for it. To develop the struggles against the evictions, for immediate unemployment relief, against high rents, discrimination, terror and persecution, etc. is still our perspective for the present time, as well as developing joint struggles of the black and white workers.

Document 7
"They Shall Not Die!"
The Liberator, June 6, 1931.

Millions of workers, colored and white, have been mobilized in the mass campaign conducted by the International Labor Defense (I.L.D.) and the League of Struggle for Negro Rights (L.S.N.R.) to save the lives of the nine innocent Negro children today facing the electric chair in the State of Alabama. Throughout the country the masses are thundering the battle-cry, THEY SHALL NOT DIE!

In thousands of meetings, in hundreds of protest parades and demonstrations, battling the bosses police who would stifle their protest against this frightful legal murder, in scores of United Front Scottsboro Defense Conferences, in increasing financial support of the defense campaign, millions of white and Negro workers have demonstrated their indignation against the murderous court room lynching planned by the Southern boss lynchers. Everywhere, both North and South, the masses are rallying to the fight against this hideous railroading to the electric chair of nine innocent boys on the trumped-up charge of "rape" against two notorious white prostitutes. Everywhere, the determined cry is being raised, THEY SHALL NOT DIE!

North and South, white and colored workers, smashing through the boss-erected barriers of race prejudice and Jim-Crowism are forcing a mighty fighting alliance to save and free these boys. A fighting alliance that says to the bloody fascist bosses, THEY SHALL NOT DIE!

And at this spectacle of the growing unity of white and black workers the imperialist bosses are becoming increasingly alarmed. The organ of the fiendish Scottsboro lynchers, the Jackson County *Sentinel*, shrieks that the mass movement to save the nine boys is:

"... THE MOST DANGEROUS MOVEMENT LAUNCHED IN THE SOUTH IN MANY YEARS!"

And the workers thunder back the fighting slogan: "THEY SHALL NOT DIE!"

This unity of the working-class, colored and white, is recognized by the bosses as a threat not only to the plans for the legal lynching of these nine youths but as a threat against the whole murderous system of Negro oppression and enslavement, against the capitalist hunger system! And the bosses are scared by that thunderous roar from the working-class, THEY SHALL NOT DIE!

This alarm of the southern boss lynchers is shared by the Negro tools and apologists of imperialism whose business of "uplifting," "advancement" (and other terms which cover up their robbery and betrayal of the Negro masses) thrives on the segregation and Jim Crowism enforced by the bosses. And they see this segregation crumbling before the advancing unity of the Negro and white masses. Thus the mass movement to save the nine boys is also seen as a dangerous movement by the treacherous leaders of the N.A.A.C.P., the servile preachers of the Chattanooga Interdenominational Ministers Alliance; the tool of the steel bosses Mr. Vann of the Pittsburgh *Courier*; the bankrupt national reformist leaders of the Garvey movement and other petty beneficiaries of the imperialist system under which the Negro masses are robbed and oppressed. These are seeking to strangle the thunderous cry rising from millions of workers throughout the land, THEY SHALL NOT DIE!

These traitors have joined with the southern boss lynchers in their attacks on the defense of the nine boys. With the most disgusting hypocrisy they are attempting to trick the Negro masses into the belief that they are defending the boys, just as they attempted, unsuccessfully, to trick the nine boys and their parents into repudiation of the I.L.D. and the mass movement which alone can save the boys, by its mass pressure on the southern courts in support of the legal defense marshaled by the I.L.D.

But that thunderous cry, THEY SHALL NOT DIE, continues to grow and spread throughout the width and breadth of the land, and is even now being taken up by tens of thousands of workers in other countries, and by the liberated millions of the Soviet Union.

Together with the white masses who are rallying to the fight to save the nine youths, the Negro masses must give increasing emphasis to the demand THEY SHALL NOT DIE! Neither the attacks of the bosses nor the treacherous activities of the Negro reformists must be permitted to prevent the growth of the mass movement to save these boys. All resistance must be swept out of the way, and with the resistance the traitors as well.

The task of saving the nine Negro boys is not only the job of the I.L.D. and the L.S.N.R. and the hundreds of organizations supporting the united front defense campaign, but the job of every individual white and Negro worker and poor farmer. Raise the question of defense in your shops, in your neighborhoods! Build block committees of 3 or 5 or 10 or more! Raise the questions of support for the defense in your organization, in your lodges, in the churches! See that your organization participates in every protest parade, in every demonstration, in every united front conference called by the I.L.D. and L.S.N.R. for the purpose of mobilizing the masses and voicing our protest against this outrage. Smash the resistance of the Uncle Tom leaders to the fight to save these boys! Expose their open cooperation with the Southern boss lynchers! See that your organization gives financial support to the International Labor Defense which is the only organization defending these boys in the boss court. Organize your own block committees, as well, and collect funds and rush them in to the International Labor Defense, 80 East 11th Street, Room 430, New York City.

Only a gigantic mass movement, only the grim resolve of the masses THEY SHALL NOT DIE can save these boys and smash the murderous frame-up against them.

Document 8
"Broaden the Mass Movement to Free the Scottsboro Boys"
    By B.D. Amis
Daily Worker, January 29, 1932.

The struggle to free the Scottsboro boys cannot be limited to the frame-work of bourgeois legality, neither can dependence be placed in Negro "leaders" to give aid in building up a united front mass defense movement.

To follow such a course is an opportunist error which will have disastrous effects upon the struggles to free the nine boys and the Negro liberation movement.

The first error is right opportunism, dependent upon legal measures, which ignores the importance of politicizing the struggle. It is a retreat to the positions of the reformists who advocate reliance upon "justice" from the courts of the lynchers. It objectively supports the base theory of these same scoundrels that a mass movement will "disturb the calm of the South and good southern race relations."

These wrong tendencies have been revealed during the course of the campaign. Their source springs from the opportunist conceptions—lack of faith in the Negro masses to struggle for immediate partial demands and against the sharpening persecution.

This lack of faith has expressed itself in the failure to build Scottsboro block and neighborhood committees. (And where they were built, to limit the struggles of the workers to the Scottsboro campaign only, no attempt being made to raise the level of the struggle and link it up with the growing waves of lynchings and increased terror against the Negro masses.) Failure to give revolutionary leadership to the militant struggles of the aroused and angered Negro masses at the present time subjects the struggles to savage verbal and physical attacks from the reformists, the capitalist class and their agents. Consequently, in the end, the struggles will be beheaded or turned into pacifist channels.

The second error is a negation of the forms of the united front tactic from below. It follows the path of least resistance, confining the struggle to a "struggle" with the Negro preachers for permission to "steal" their carefully guarded congregations from before their eyes. It is an attempt to build a united front from the top, to follow in the tail of the misleaders, who stand ready to serve their class interests and not the interests of the Negro toilers.

The leftist mistake to limit the struggle to the acts of a few revolutionary mass organizations places the campaign on a narrow sectarian base. The wrong conception of winning freedom for the boys (only adopting protest resolutions and sending protest telegrams) without the aid of outside pressure from the Negro masses and white and colored workers fails to broaden the united front. Rarely has the struggle been concretely linked up to the every day struggles of the workers for partial demands.

How to Avoid Mistakes

How can we best overcome such opportunistic errors? The comrades in the suburban town of Detroit, Hamtramck, have set a good example as to how to broaden out the struggle by correctly linking it up with the election and unemployment campaigns. The demonstration of workers before the town council produced sufficient mass pressure to force the City Council to send a protest telegram to the governor of Alabama, denouncing this hideous frame-up. Other cities must follow this good example by mobilizing masses of whites and Negroes to demonstrate before the city councils in their respective cities and demand that they too should take the same action. Especially should demonstrations be held before the homes of Negro politicians such as Aldermen of Negro Wards. Mass pressure will force them to declare themselves on the case and growing Negro persecutions. We must demand of them to accede to the pressure of the indignant masses and send protest telegrams to the Alabama state officials. Their failure to do so gives us an opportunity to expose them before the Negro masses and brand them for what they are—class enemies to the struggle to free the nine boys and to the Negro liberation movement.

We must appeal over the heads of the Negro reformists to their rank and file membership. Their treachery and class interest must be exposed and they must be isolated from the rank and file who are willing and ready to struggle. Building block and neighborhood committees is a method to reach the rank and file members of the reformist organization. Street demonstrations in the Negro neighborhoods and before local politicians will draw into the struggle the most conscious sections of the Negro masses. Appeals to the membership of workers' clubs should be made. Such forms of activities take us away from running around to churches and bring us in direct contact with the toiling masses.

The slogans issued on Scottsboro, appearing in the *Daily Worker*, January 20, 1932, will (with our concrete agitation) awaken the political consciousness of the Negro masses and white workers to intensify the struggle and raise it to a higher political level. Masses of Negroes and whites must be drawn into such a program to produce required results and to broaden out the struggles.

We must smash through the subtle frame-work of bourgeois legality with a tremendous out-pouring of proletarian protests and demonstrations. Such activities will draw into the struggle those organizations and sections of the masses which are not on the periphery of our movement. It will turn the extensive indignation of the Negro masses into real revolutionary channels of struggle and will afford us an opportunity to build our organizations. The fact must not be minimized that the form of struggle as applied in Hantramck is one that will give to the toiling masses a weapon which will be decisive in aiding to smash the power which holds the nine innocent boys.

The immediate danger which confronts us is that the struggle will not assume the broad character that it should and that while waiting for the decision of the Alabama Supreme Court, a lull will set in, which will enable the southern lynch bosses to carry through their plans of legal lynching unnoticed by the international and American toiling masses. Effective mass action, broadening out the struggle (at the same time properly linking it up to the struggle for partial demands), increasing its power, and always bearing in mind that the boys will burn if we are not alert to keep the masses. ·

CHAPTER 5
SPEECHES OF B. D. AMIS

Speech Nominating William Z. Foster
for President of the United States
[Chicago Convention of the CPUSA, May 29, 1932]

Comrades, Friends, and Fellow-workers:

This convention will mark a historical milestone in the struggle of the American workers and poor farmers, against their oppressors, the capitalist class. To the bourgeoisie and imperialists, they will more plainly see the hand-writing on the wall—the revolutionizing the struggles of the toiling masses and their steeled determination to put an end to capitalism under the revolutionary leadership of our Communist Party.

American capitalism is in a deep crisis. The poverty and misery of the working population is worsening. The 15,000,000 jobless workers are being plunged into demoralization by a rapidly decaying system of society. The low level standards of living of the millions of part-time workers are being lowered with lightning rapidity. General wage cuts in steel, railroads and other industries give full endorsement to the Hoover program of starvation by the capitalist robbers. The life savings of millions of poor workers have been squandered by greedy scoundrels, through numerous bank crashes. The poor farmers are forced to see food stuffs stolen from them by the profiteers rot in the warehouses. There is no relief in sight. "Prosperity" to the workers and poor farmers is a lying phrase to be associated with the imperialist bandits, Hoover, Mellon, Rockefeller, etc..

This savage offensive of the imperialists is not only limited to an attack on the economic standards of the workers but is extended to a vile onslaught on the political rights of the masses.

Increased political reaction of the bourgeoisie is shown in their failure to give immediate relief and unemployment and social insurance as demanded by the National Hunger March to Washington at the expense of the state and the employers, to the jobless millions—by the bloody slaughter of who dare to fight against evictions and demand instant relief. (This was shown in Chicago where three Negro workers were killed and Melrose Park where the employed were stood up against a wall as cattle and mowed down with machine gun fire, in Detroit where the Ford-Murphy machine snuffed out the lives of four workers in a demonstration that demanded relief for the former Ford workers, in Cleveland where two Negroes were murdered for protecting against eviction. The persecution against the foreign-born has been unleashed in all its fury, (Edith Berkman, etc.) by the continued imprisonment of Tom Mooney with the support of the Hoover administration and the A.F. of L. leaders.

The imperialists of the world are feverishly preparing for a new war—a slaughter of the workers and poor farmers and an attack against the Soviet Union and the partition of China. In this mad rush to seize more booty, Japanese imperialism, with the moral sanction of the League of Nations, is the spearhead of aggressive action. American imperialism gives its support through the shipping of war materials and ammunition to Japan and by passively consenting to the rape of Manchuria, the slaughter of the Shanghai workers and the mobilizing of thousands of Japanese soldiers on the Soviet frontier. Our Party mobilizes the American toilers to give stubborn resistance to these planned attacks against the Soviet Union to answer—that capitalism will break its teeth on the iron stronghold of socialist construction because the American proletariat together with the international proletariat will intervene. Such intervention will express solidarity of action and will help strengthen the Red Army, the buttress of defense to the Soviet Union population.

To carry out this policy of war and of attack against the workers the bourgeoisie is building up its third party, the Socialist Party, in view of the fast waning of influence and loss of confidence in the two major parties, Republican and Democratic. The fast radicalization of the masses indicates that the Republican and Democratic parties can no longer quell their profound discontentment. Therefore capitalism finds it expedient to bolster up the Socialist Party in order to use these social fascist leaders as a means of turning the militant upsurge of the masses into channels unharmful to the capitalists. Also, there is a deliberate attempt to revive the fast disintegrating A. F. of L. officialdom, as manifested in the Penn-Ohio coal miners strike. This gesture has only a purpose to betray striker's struggles and to confuse the struggling workers and prevent their joining militant Red Trade Unions.

In the face of this increased political reaction the workers and poor farmers are looking for a way out. There is a way out—a revolutionary way out—under the leadership of our Party. The workers and peasants of the Soviet Union have blazed the trail. The building up of socialism and the completion of the Five Year Plan place the Soviet Union as a monument, towering mightily over the capitalist world and calling to the exploited and oppressed people to follow in their footsteps to give active support to the Communist election platform of immediate demands.

It is in such a situation that our Party puts forward a program of class against class—of war to the end for the overthrow of capitalism. Therefore to lead these gigantic struggles—to become the symbol and standard bearer of the fight against capitalism, to force the bourgeoisie to grant concessions to the workers—I nominate for president on the Communist Party ticket a steel worker, one who has been a foremost fighter for Negro rights, and for self-determination in the Black Belt—one who has bitterly denounced the Hoover starvation program—one who has exposed the bureaucrats in the A. F. of L.—one who has rooted himself deep in the proletariat as a leader of the great steel strike in 1919—of the Penn-Ohio, West Virginia and Kentucky coal strike of 40,000 and 10,000 respectively, of the 10,000 textile workers in Lawrence; as an outstanding fighter for the freedom of the Scottsboro boys, Tom Mooney, Edith Berkman, etc., for these reasons which prove his ability to lead the workers today in deadly struggle against war and capitalism—to show the revolutionary way out of the crisis—I nominate William Z. Foster.

Radio Speech of B. D. Amis, Candidate for Auditor-General, State of Pennsylvania, Station WGAL

[Lancaster, PA, September 30, 1936]

FOR A FREE, HAPPY AND PROSPEROUS AMERICA!

This election year presents the American people with many serious and important problems. We have been asked to either uphold the traditions of our great people in meeting these problems or to repudiate these traditions.

We have to decide whether we shall live in a free happy and prosperous country, whether we shall be rid of mass unemployment, worsening working conditions and whether labor shall have the right to organize for better conditions without interference, or whether we shall have the sinister shadow of reaction and terror hanging over our heads, which impede the progress of society.

In the past period labor has made many gains. There is a progressive spirit in the labor movement. Millions of the common people are moving in the direction which shall assure their emancipation from political and economic slavery. A great task facing organized labor today is to organize the great mass of workers in the mass production industries and at the same time steer these workers into channels of independent political action as the best guarantee that their standards of living shall not be lowered.

This necessitates a unified and strong labor movement. The menace of the Hearst-Liberty League groups to our civil liberties and democratic rights stands before us as a vicious monster ready to seize upon its prey. These enemies of labor have their candidate Landon who is the representative of the concentration of the most reactionary and outspoken enemies of the common people. They stand for a decisive change in meeting the problems of today. They are for the adopting of those dictator methods similarly used in Germany and Italy. This means mass misery and suffering, curbing the rights of the people and their organizations and increasing the riches of the privileged class. We do not want mass unemployment. We do not want to suffer and see our children denied the right to have all the conveniences of life. We want more wages and better working conditions. We want the right to enjoy the fruits of our labor. But Landon and the Republican Party do not offer this. Look at the 5000 children who are the innocent sufferers of that dreadful disease silicoses in the state of Kansas where Landon is governor! Consider the plan of these men to throw all off the relief rolls when stubborn and unyielding industrial and financial magnates refuse to give employment to 11,000,000 jobless without having first the guarantee that their profits shall soar a hundred per cent. Their talk is idle chatter.

It is to this group of labor haters that the notorious judge B.C. Atlee, has a close tie-up. He expresses the philosophy of these people on a local scale. It was he who wished to bring into the atmosphere of this fair city a lynching hysteria by his recommendation of the chain gang and by his declaration of endorsement of the rope and faggot, which are known past-times of the lynch-terror-South, when a Negro was brought before him to be sentenced.

H.W. Prentice, Jr., head of the Armstrong Cork Co., a known member of the Liberty-Leaguers and better known for his record against organized labor, together with Judge Atlee constitute a serious menace to the liberty-loving people of this vicinity. Because the Republican Party has within its ranks similar individuals it is imperative that the common people must organize a united front for the defeat of Landon and the driving out of office of the little Landons and all those who express their ideas.

Roosevelt and the Democratic Party waver between reaction and democracy. When pressure from the progressives is applied Roosevelt grants concessions to labor, but when the reactionaries of Wall St. and the U.S. Chamber of Commerce and other similar organizations apply their pressures, Roosevelt yields. The president submitted to the dictates of the U.S. Supreme Court, labor legislation was nullified, such as the labor codes, the Guffey Coal Act, the farmers' AAA etc.. No word of protest came from Roosevelt in the interest of the common people in defense of their fundamental rights. Consequently, Roosevelt and his party which attempt to follow a middle course, can not be depended upon as a barrier to fascism and reaction.

Lemke, the candidate of the Union Party, is a stooge for Landon. He is being used by Coughlin and Hearst to divert people disillusioned with the failure of the New Deal to carry out its promises into reactionary channels. Lemke makes feeble and vague promises to attract the farmers and workers. He is silent on the question of higher wages, on the right of trade unions to organize, on relief for the unemployed, on old age pensions and on help to the poor farmers. This stand of Lemke is caused for the repudiation of his candidacy by many of the outstanding Farm organizations. It can plainly be seen that Lemke does not represent the interest of labor but that he is being used as bait to catch the votes of that discontented section of the population to make more easy the election of Landon.

The Communist Party stands squarely for the rights of labor to organize and strike. We stand for the right of the toiling people to defend their democratic rights which have been won through bitter struggles against an oppressing class. We stand for the right to develop that independent political action of labor which shall express itself into the form of the Farmer-Labor Party. This Farmer-Labor Party shall be the American Peoples Front. It must be an anti-fascist front, a movement against war. It must be a promoter of progressive trade unionism such as the building of industrial unions and the organizing of the large mass of unorganized workers in the mass production industries. This Farmer-Labor Party must support the demands of the unemployed workers for unemployment insurance and old age security. It must become the guarantee to preserve the civil rights of the people. We support such a broad movement because first it is progressive, and secondly, millions of the American people are moving into the arena of progressive action and want these concessions. The granting of these concessions is a guarantee against the growth of reaction and fascism.

The Communist Party states that the rich must be made to pay for the mass misery and suffering that they have thrust upon the common people. We demand the opening of the closed factories as the American people need all of the products of our industries. The government must open and operate these factories, mills and mines for the benefit of the people, if the private employers refuse to do so. The productive powers and industries of our nation must be used to give every working man, woman and child a decent standard of living.

We demand legislation which shall provide security for the jobless and the aged. An adequate system of social insurance for the unemployed, the disabled, the sick as provided in the Frazier-Lundeen Bill is a demand which must become the law of the land. We are for the increase in the relief standards. We state stop the relief cuts, stop playing with the misery of the unemployed. The farmers must be freed from debts, unbearable tax burdens and foreclosures. The American government is obligated to save the American farmers from distress and ruin. It must guarantee them the right to the land which they till. Immediate relief must be given to the farmers by the government to prevent the large holding companies and corporations from robbing them of their land. The small farmer should be exempted from taxation during this period of depression. We are against the curtailment and destruction of crops. We favor that the government should regulate the farm prices in order to give a guarantee to the farmer that he shall make the cost of production.

Our Party states that the dictatorial and usurped powers of the U.S. Supreme Court should be ended and that Congress which is the representative expression of the people should reassert its constitutional powers and enact social and labor legislation to curb the U.S. Supreme Court. We champion those rights of the people which they have won in the glorious struggles of 1776 and 1861. We are for the full enforcing of the Equal Rights Bill which up to the present time has been used as a boomerang against the colored people of this Commonwealth. We are against every form of Jim-crowism, discrimination and segregation. Those who violate the right of the colored must be punished by law in the payment of heavy fines or by long term imprisonment. The Negro people must be guaranteed complete equality, the right to have all jobs receiving equal pay, the right to enter all public places free from insults and intimidations and the right to educational facilities.

I ask the people to vote for the Communist candidate, Earl Browder for president. James W. Ford for vice-president, Pat Toohey for State Treasurer, B.D. Amis for Auditor General, J. Granville Eddy for Congress, Harry Davis for State Assembly, these gentlemen are the true representatives of the people. They are the outstanding fighters for the Farmer-Labor Party. They represent the true Americans of today. They are the continuators of those traditions that our forefathers who in the heroic battles of 1776 and 1861 established the right that the people of America shall be free from the yoke of oppression, established the right that our people shall dwell in peace and prosperity. The right of the American people to enjoy liberty, security and progress is what we Communists demand. This is Americanism. We Communists love our country, we are not the destroyers. It is Hearst and the fascists who are the savages who would wreck our civilization. Communism means a free, happy and prosperous America. Communism is twentieth-century Americanism. Vote Communist as the best guarantee for the maintenance of those rights that we now enjoy, as the guarantee for securing additional rights, as the guarantee that the peoples movement, the Farmer-Labor Party shall be built in this country as a barrier to the growth of reaction and fascism.

The press has flashed the news today that reaction has again raised its ugly head in Terre Haute, Ind. Earl Browder, Communist candidate for president, together with Waldo Frank, a novelist of New York, and Seymour Waldman, a journalist, were arrested by the chief of police, James C. Yates and held to prevent the holding of an election campaign rally. This is a concrete example of the denial of the right to free speech, the right of assembly;

it is an example of the growth of reaction and the flagrant violation of the fundamental rights won in struggle by the American people. It is a violation of our constitutional rights. I appeal to my listeners and to all lovers of liberty to denounce and protest this vicious action. Send your protest to the president at the White House, and to Governor Paul V. McNutt, Indianapolis, Indiana, or to the chief of police, James C. Yates, Terre Haute, demanding the right for people who desire to hear the truth.

Vote Communist!

Radio Speech of B. D. Amis, Candidate for Auditor-General, State of Pennsylvania, Station WIP
[Philadelphia, October 22, 1936]

AN APPEAL TO THE COLORED VOTERS TO VOTE COMMUNIST.

My Friends and Fellow-citizens:

It is indeed a pleasure to address you tonight on the issues of this very important election campaign.

Seldom have the people and especially my people, the Negro people, been asked to uphold those traditions for which this nation was established. Those traditions of democracy, peace, happiness and prosperity are of paramount importance today. These are the questions that we must decide on November 3rd .

At present the sinister monster of reaction cloaked in the Black Legion, the Ku Klux Klan and vigilantes threatens our democratic rights and institutions. My people have cause for alarm. We have experienced time and again the terror and violence and all the horrors that accompany every action of these super-imposed authorities which seek to crush our liberty with the rope and faggot and with the unwritten law of segregation and discrimination.

During its many years in office, the Republican Party has hypocritically posed as the friend of the Negro people.

It was the Liberty-Leaguers, Grundy, Pew, Wir & Co. who were responsible in directing the policy of the State Republican Senators who for more than three weeks last summer held up all relief funds. It was these same people who cut, by ten million dollars, the inadequate amount of relief proposed by the Democrats. It was the Republican Party which excluded Negroes from hearing Landon's speech at Middlesex, Pa. by issuing cards of admission to "Whites Only."

It was the Republican Party that jim-crowed the Negroes at the Landon notification in Topeka, Kansas. Landon, the figure-head of Hearst and the Republican Party, is notoriously prejudiced against the colored people. It was he who turned out of the State House, when he became governor of Kansas, all Negroes employed by the government who received more than $100 per month. He fostered the policy of anti-Semitism in the hospitals.

In our state, the infamous Judge B.C. Atlee of Lancaster, in the case of a Negro, Samuel Watson, declared, "It is no credit to the people of Columbia that they allowed you here (i.e. in court) today. Had they lynched you, they would have been justified. It is most fortunate for you that this offense occurred north of the Mason and Dixon Line. No court has to bother with cases of your kind south of that line." This statement is not only an insult to my people but to the whole people. It is a blot upon the fair name of this great commonwealth. It is a call to Lynch Law. It is a plea to incite the hoodlum elements to ignore constituted law and to become the exponents of mob rule. Such labor haters and blood-thirsty lynchers infest the Republican Party. This is the party of Wall Street, of the Liberty-Leaguers, of Hearst, the foremost enemy of the American people. The Republican Party is chained to the wheels of the worst Negro-haters. It can no longer champion the rights of the colored people. By its actions it gives encouragement to the Black Legion and the Ku Klux Klan. He who supports such a Party is helping to enslave my people—is helping to put a rope around our necks.

The Republican Party of today is not the party of Lincoln, the great emancipator, who championed the rights of the down-trodden people.

The Democratic Party and Roosevelt are making serious efforts to get the votes of the colored people. They have made a few concessions. But how can my people forget that this party which has its base of power in the South is the party of Southern Lynchers, is the party which keeps thousands of my people in a condition of servitude, is the party of the most brutal backward aristocracy of the South.

The streets of Washington, D.C. have been spattered with the blood of 20 innocent Negroes since December 24, 1933, by the savage shootings by policemen. Not one of these brutal murders was investigated. Full responsibility for this condition rests upon Superintendent of Police, Major Ernest Brown, appointee of the Roosevelt administration and with the Democratic Congress which supervises the government of the District of Columbia.

In spite of the fact that Governor Earle signed the Equal Rights Bill, every case tested to punish the violators of this bill, has been used against the offended person.

A cynical judge or a prejudiced court has always added additional insult by permitting the transgressor to go scott free, and at times, causing the Negro to pay the costs of court.

With the blessings of the Democratic Party in the South, trade union organizers, liberal investigators of the plantation system, and colored sharecroppers have been whipped, tarred and feathered, and run out of town. In the South, my people know this Party as the Party of the Night-Riders, the Party of the Ku Klux Klan, the Party of the Black Terror.

The Democratic majority in the house at Harrisburg developed an un-canny silence against the mass movement which was started for the im-peachment of the would-be lynch-law, Judge Atlee.

The long years of the Republican rule in Philadelphia have given to my people the worst slum areas in the world. A British housing expert, complet-ing a survey of housing, declared, "that Philadelphia was the cite of the worst slums in the country." The average age of houses occupied by colored people was 53.7 years old compared with 32.7 for those occupied by whites. The percentage of structures requiring structural repairs or unfit for use was 23% as opposed to 5.2% for white housing. 21.1% colored homes are with-out baths, 19.6% are without toilets. 6.5% have no gas and 7.7% have no electricity. Is it any wonder that the death rate among the colored people is three times greater than that among the whites and that 170 out of every 10,000 Negroes dies of tuberculosis as opposed of 45 out of every 10,000 whites? During the most important period of learning years 6-10, 1239 pu-pils in the Fifth School District are deprived of necessary training. This school district is predominantly colored and 30 out of 50 part-time classes are in the Reynolds and Singerly Schools, where the children receive twenty hours instruction per week or ten hours less than other children.

Colored men and women cannot secure a shelter in either of the two major parties, which carry out the policy opposed to their manhood and womanhood rights. These parties deprive us of those vital things necessary to a happy life, and spurn the consistent violations of the 13th, 14th and 15th amendments to the Constitution. They place us upon the burning alter as an extra sacrifice to appease their gods of super-profit and oppression.

It is to be regretted that we have leaders within our own ranks who are hog-tied to these political machines. They do a great disservice to the libera-tion struggles of my people.

The issues in this campaign are quite clear. Are we to support either directly or indirectly the forces of reaction, those forces that retard the pro-gress of humanity as represented by Hearst and Landon, or those forces which attempt to satisfy everyone and satisfy no one as represented by Roo-sevelt? Or, are we going to take independent political action and unite with the progressive people who are striving for a peaceful and happy life?

It should be clear to all that the latter is the course. The support of my people must go to help build the Farmer-Labor Party, the People's Front as a barrier to reaction and the rapacious policies of Wall Street and its agents.

The Union Party, inspired by Father Coughlin, an American admirer of Hitler, Nazi methods, is the embodiment in a compact form of a group of rabid Negro-haters.

The Communist Party stands squarely for the rights of labor to organize and strike. It stands for the right of the toiling people to defend their democ-ratic rights which have been won through bitter struggles against an oppres-sive class. We stand for the full rights of the Negro people. Plank 7 of our

Election Platform states: "We demand that the Negro people be guaranteed complete equality, equal rights to jobs, equal pay for equal work, the full right to organize, vote, serve on juries and hold public office. Segregation and public discrimination against Negroes must be declared a crime. Heavy penalties must be established against mob rule, floggers, and kidnappers with the death penalty for lynchers. We demand the enforcement of the 13th, 14th, and 15th amendments to the Constitution."

Our Presidential standard-bearer, Earl Browder, has shown the way to cement the unity of the toiling white population and the Negro people. It was he who, when the hotel managements of Philadelphia and Baltimore, insulted my people, defiantly protested against this flagrant violation of the rights of mankind, the rights of the Negro people, by checking out of the hotel, calling off a press conference and going to those places where he was assured that colored reporters would receive equal treatment accorded to whites. Compare this to the record of Landon at the Topeka Notification, at the Middlesex meeting, compare this to the slanderous slimy remarks of the Democratic Senator, who, when our own colored minister offered a prayer, a plea for justice and righteousness, at the opening of the Democratic National Convention, walked out of the Hall.

My Party champions those rights of the people which they won in the glorious struggles of 1776 and 1861. My Party champions those traditions of Thomas Jefferson, Abraham Lincoln and Frederick Douglas. My Party champions those hallowed words that flowed from the tongue of the Great Emancipator, "This country and its institutions belong to the people," but who are the people? The millions of toilers whose sweat and blood has enriched the coffers of the parasites who, in winter, go to the sun-kissed shores of Florida and in the summer to the rockbound coast of Maine, and the wooded-arcadias of Canada. These are the people, that important tenth of the population, the colored people, they too are the people. But the 400 families which rule America conveniently forget that this important tenth which lives in the slum areas, which is denied even the elementary democratic rights enjoyed by the white people, which is subjected to every insult, every atrocity that is created by the degenerated elements of society, has the right to live as human beings, and that this country and its institutions also belong to them. The white people cannot hope to defend their democratic rights and liberty and to gain greater security in life, as long as the Negro people are subject to a cruel and inhuman system which consistently oppresses them.

In this campaign, the Communist Party raises the slogan, "The right of the people to decide against an oppressing bureaucracy." This is the main question that was raised by Jefferson against the yoke of George III. He was branded as a traitor. Lincoln raised it against the slave barons. He was branded as a Tory. Our Party raises this slogan against the Mellons, the Fords, the Grundys and the Pews, the Rockefellers, and Hearsts brands us un-American. But if to be a fighter for the rights of my people, if to demand justice, a living wage and decent relief for the unemployed, if to unite with the progressive forces that are against war and fascism and are for raising the level of the whole toiling population, if this provokes the wrath of the Hearsts and the Liberty-Leaguers, let us make the most of it. We are fighting for Americanism. This is Communism.

I ask my people to vote the full Communist ticket, Earl Browder for President, James W. Ford for Vice-President, Pat Toohey for State Treasurer, B.D. Amis for Auditor-General. These gentlemen are true representatives of the people. They are the outstanding fighters for the People's Front, the Farmer-Labor Party. They represent progressive trade unionism. They are the known fighters for the freedom of the Scottsboro boys and Angelo Herndon. They represent the true Americans of today. They are the continuators of those great traditions that our forefathers who in the heroic battles of 1776 and 1861 established the right of the American people to enjoy liberty and security.

We Communists demand this. This is Americanism. Hearst and the Fascists are the barbarians who seek to wreck our civilization. Communism means a free, happy and prosperous America.

Join our Party. Write for copies of literature and our Election Platform to 62 N. 8 Street, Philadelphia, Pa.

VOTE COMMUNIST!

CHAPTER 6
CLEVELAND DISTRICT
ORGANIZER [1933]

Excerpts from "Report E.C.C.I./Situation and Tasks of the American Party and the Cleveland District" at Anglo-American Secretariat Meeting, April 2, 1933.

Comrades, in my report I want to elaborate upon a few points mentioned in the report of Comrade Browder and speak on some of the experiences and difficulties in the shop, trade union, and unemployed work in the Cleveland district. Also, if time permits, I will give a few interesting facts about our work in other fields.

Comrade Browder spoke about the numerical decline in the shop units. As true as this is I would like to focus the attention upon our small beginnings in the building up of the united front in certain shops in the automobile and steel plants and the methods of work used which were a decided change from the old and have produced already some organization and struggles.

The fierce attacks of the bourgeoisie upon the living standards of the workers are felt most keenly by the workers in the shops thru numerous wage cuts, the stagger system, and the speed-up. The influence of industrial capital and the constant contraction of markets (a part of the general crisis) forces the bourgeoisie to seek this way out. At present, thousands of part time workers, working one, two, and four days a month, having their pay checks robbed regularly for so called insurance dues and supplies are little better off than the totally unemployed. In the face of this terrible onslaught there is a deep going radicalization and an increasing will to struggle.

However, the Party is just beginning, in the real sense of the word, to orientate to shop work. As weak as this work is, it would be incorrect to underestimate some serious attempts to root ourselves among the factory workers, especially in the auto, steel and metal industries, two highly trustified industries which had not before yielded to strike struggles from the pressure of the crisis.

The strikes developed and led by us in the industries can be attributed to shop activities—to concentrate on selected plants by district functionaries, together with section and unit forces—to a drastic change in our methods of work—to the beginning to work down below to build up the united front. Also the holding of the eastern and mid-western shop conferences provided a rich exchange of experience and helped to establish a better understanding of how to carry on this important work. These conferences, in my opinion, can be considered an advance in registering new experiences and forms of ___ going on in the Party.

What are some of the methods used? First our comrades took concentration more seriously after the 14th CC Plenum. Shop work was not limited to a shop unit in a given plant or to a few selected comrades, but it became the task of the district organizer and other leading comrades. But it became the task of the district organizer and other leading comrades who worked closely and quite regularly with the section forces and street units shop comrades and some of the language organizations. In the auto industry, work was started on the outside of the plant. Workers were visited in their homes, small group meetings of two-eight were called in the neighborhoods. Others were reached thru the mass organizations and thru their friends. Social affairs were held, reading classes and sport activity were established. In some cases, our comrades became officers in some of the clubs and lived the same life of and with the workers. It was found out that the workers were interested in various things and by taking up these activities and becoming part and parcel of the daily lives of the workers, we gained their confidence and created a precondition to talk about the conditions in their shop or if they happened to be unemployed to get them to acquaint us with their friends who were drawn into the clubs and small meetings.

In one case a comrade working in a steel plant, won the confidence of his shop mates by daily giving them apples for their lunches. This comrade was an Italian worker, but he was able to bring into the union American workers. In another, a comrade started a checker club among some American workers. Thru this effort, eight workers came to our meeting.

The unemployed workers have been of great help in giving us contact with workers employed, also they have gone visiting these workers with our comrades. In the Fisher Body plant, Cleveland, the unemployed workers, after receiving news of a wage cut in the glue department from our shop comrades, held a shop gate meeting and distributed a special leaflet on the Detroit strike and its lessons to the workers in this department. The wage cut was immediately rescinded and a two to three cents increase on the hour was given. In Canton our comrades organized a committee of five unemployed workers to demand relief for a steel worker who had lost his job in the Central Alloy (Republic) plant. The first visit of the committee to the charity was unsuccessful. On the second visit, ten workers went down. Relief was won. This attracted the workers in the shop who began to demand that the discharged one should be given work. A small committee was set up on the inside; it became a union group of fifteen members; it continued the work started and after a month the worker was given back his job. Such methods of work are the beginning of the building up of the united front. They give us an opportunity to learn the issues and problems facing the workers and prepare the way for bigger actions.

At the announcement of the Community Fund Drive to be started in the steel plants in Youngstown, we called together our shop group in the Carnegie mill. These comrades were all Spanish speaking and knew very little English. But we asked questions of them on how we could get the workers together or to talk to them that they should not give to the fund. Our comrades were not able to give us any information. We suggested that each comrade should speak to the worker next to him, saying that our wages are so small that we can't give; we have too large families; we need to help ourselves; let's tell the foreman. In the department only Spanish and Polish men worked. The comrades, speaking very poor English, were able to make the Polish workers understand. Everyone in the department refused to give when they came around to collect. No one was fired. In the other departments of the mill all of the workers contributed.

We obtained 3-400 contacts of miners in the Hocking Valley area during the election campaign. Our candidates spoke in meeting of 8-900 miners, who were willing to accept our program of struggle, in part, since they had been betrayed so many times by the AFL officialdom. The result was that these miners wrote to the district office and to the Hungarian paper, *Uj Elore*, demanding that we send in an organizer. Of course we should have not waited for them to have written. But they have given us the base to organize mine units of unemployed miners and build opposition groups inside of the AFL. Already we have established a good group among the Hungarians and have held a two weeks school of about twenty of these miners.

In Farrel, Pa., we established a union group in the mill of seven comrades by holding an unemployed demonstration in spite of great terror. The response to our demands of the unemployed was proven in the turning out of 400 workers who fought with the police. After this, our comrades approached some workers who before had refused to talk about the union. This time they said that the union was helping the unemployed steel workers so it must be a good union.

The auto strike and the one strike in steel were largely prepared by the shop comrades who used these forms of work. *The role of the shop unit in strike struggles is of great importance in the preparatory and organizational stages.* Despite the many handicaps and poor methods of work, the foreign born composition, etc., the Warren Republic nucleus took a great part in the

building of the Steel and Metal Workers Industrial Union. It created an ideological base in the mill for the union; it carried on recruiting and was the
main instrument thru which we sent our literature into the plant. Together
with the union we led a strike. The same can be said in varying degrees of
the shop units in the Ford plants.

What retards our building organization in the shops? The chief obstacles, in my opinion, are, 1. our lack of knowledge of how to go about this
work; 2. our sectarian approach to the workers. We have not learned the best
form of conspiritive work, which would protect our contacts from the bosses
and their spies

"Next Steps in the Struggles for Winter Relief"

(1933 Document, Amis Papers)

Communist Party of the USA District Six
1245 Prospect Ave.
Cleveland, Ohio

To the Fraction of the Unemployed Council
To the Unit Members
To the Fraction and Language Secretaries

Dear Comrades:

The national hunger march had a far reaching political effect upon the
broadest masses of workers. It has brought more sharply forward the deep
radicalization that is taking place, the growing reaction of the bourgeoisie
and the acceptance by the broadest masses of workers the Party's revolutionary program of struggle as the only way out of the pauper-stricken conditions. This march has brought out very plainly the outstanding fact that concessions can be rung from the government and the bourgeoisie. The retreat
of the Washington government in the face of stubborn resistance and the
determined demands of the 3000 delegates backed up by the masses of
workers is proof that the struggle for partial demands is the key to revolutionizing the struggles of the American working class. Therefore without
going into the weaknesses and shortcomings of the march, it is necessary
that we must proceed with all haste to take advantage of the ripeness of the
workers to struggle for winter relief.

Utilization of the Marchers

You have already received directives on what is to be done to get the best services out of the marchers. We wish to add the following:

1. At the section buros and units, thru the fraction of the unemployed block committees, we shall work closely to set up in each respective territory (section, unit, block and neighborhood council territories) a schedule of meetings at which the delegates shall make their report on the march.

2. Special comrades (marchers) should be assigned to key points for concentration work in the units, sections or block committees for an indefinite period to build up:
   a. Struggle in the local territories against the local politicians and the charity organizations.
   b. To develop new forces to become leaders in the unemployed struggle.
   c. To recruit these good elements into the Party.

3. Delegates shall be assigned to report to the members in the language and mass organizations which shall hold special meetings for these occasions.

4. The most outstanding of the marchers shall be called to the Unemployed Council committees and shall receive special instructions on the type of reports that they shall give and shall be sent to AF of L locals, shop groups, organizations under reactionary leadership, etc. Special house meetings shall be held as well. Special meetings in the territories inviting workers from the factories, steel mills, shops and miners. Youth marchers shall be sent to specially arranged youth meetings.

5. The character of these reports should stress:
   a. The militancy and determination of the marchers to endure all the rigors in order to present the demands of the 15,000 unemployed to Congress.
   b. The organized nation wide terror initiated from Washington which had its purpose to crush the struggles of the unemployed.
   c. The wonderful response and reception of the workers in the cities, towns, villages, country sides to the marchers and their demonstrative solidarity.
   d. The united front character of the march which contained workers from organized groups (mass organizations, AF of L locals, trade unions, SP workers, CP workers, etc. Negro, women, and youth who united to struggle for the single purpose of winter relief and for unemployment insurance at the expense of the bosses and federal government.
   e. The role of the political parties guided by Wall street who put every obstacle in the path of the marchers to keep them from achieving their aims

as contrasted to the role of the CP in this big movement. The traitorous role of the SP lied about the real facts of the march. At the most opportune time in the speech the role of the CP should be brought forward.

f. The demagogy of the city administration and their close collaboration with the Washington government and being forced to feed and lodge the marchers. (Rotten food in Cleveland).

g. The necessity for building up the broadest united front form of struggle as the only solution to obtaining more benefits for the employed and unemployed workers.

6. The section and unit buros together with the district buro thru selection of the fraction in unemployed work shall be responsible for developing a group of marchers for leading work in the unemployed field, trade union and the Party.

a. The names and addresses of these marchers are to be submitted to the district.

b. Special attention shall be given them in the form of personal instructions from the buro and leading comrades and by sending them to schools which should be in the process of opening. If they are not under way they must be established at once.

c. The comrades to be selected shall be the ones who have proved in the course of the march their ability under fire to give leadership and showed aggressiveness and revolutionary potentialities and capability of understanding the revolutionary program of struggle whether or not they are Party members.

7. At all of these meetings the proper literature such as the leaflets on the fight for unemployment insurance and winter relief, the pamphlet, "Why We March," the *Daily Worker*, etc. must be broadly distributed and the work of the fraction must become the outstanding factor in broadening out the Party base among the unemployed and carrying forth a bold recruiting campaign.

8. Special efforts must be made to organize meetings in remote territories such as small villages and farm territories, etc. where we have no organization. The marcher delegate shall be sent there to carry on this work. For such work, it should be well to look up the contacts that were sent from time to time from the district of workers who have purchased literature and have made inquiries of the Party and unemployed work. These contacts will give us the opportunity to carry out such activities.

9. Public meetings and open hearings should be held at which the marcher delegate will speak. To such meetings local officials should be invited to give an answer to the questions raised by the delegates to the demands of the unemployed in that neighborhood.

10. At the house meetings, after the report of the marchers and discussions, block committees should be elected to carry out the following tasks in order to become the economic factors and permanent organs of struggle in their community.

a. To carry on an investigation regards the needs of families, school children; to investigate the salaries of neighborhood officials, and the amount of money given for neighborhood enterprises and the distribution of work in the neighborhood.

b. To call neighbors to protest and demand relief for the needy cases from the local politicians, charities, board of education, etc.

c. To initiate struggles against evictions, cutting off of water, etc.

d. To carry on cultural activities to keep alive the committees when they are not engaged in struggle; plays, parties, lectures, first aid medical courses, training classes for children, etc.

11. An appeal for funds must always be made to help to continue the struggle.

The purpose of all these plans is to stir the masses into a mighty mass action, to build up a united front of struggle, to build up permanent organs of struggle, block committees and unemployed councils, to sharply expose the role of the bourgeois politicians, the social fascists, the reactionary leaders, to point out the unfitness of the capitalist society to serve the needs and demands of the workers; to build up the unemployed council, to recruit new members into the Party and to develop new revolutionary fighters.

Every unit and section must work out a concrete plan and send it into the district. Weekly reports must be sent in by these organs into the district.

This plan must be discussed in each unit and section buro and concretized to the local situation. The fractions in the mass organizations must follow the same line; that is they must meet regularly to plan and check up the work and are responsible to get results in their respective organizations.

Comradely yours,
DISTRICT SERCRETARIAT
B.D. Amis

CHAPTER 7
INTERNATIONAL PRESS CORRE-SPONDENCE ESSAYS

The National Recovery Act Lynch Drive Calls for Mass Resistance
By B.D. Amis
International Press Correspondence, February 9, 1934.

The "New Deal" to the Negro masses was the same old deal in disguise. N.R.A. became the symbol, "Negro Repressive Act,"—"No Rights At All." In the industries that predominantly employ Negro workers, the N.R.A. operated in a repressive manner. Wage rates were generally omitted from the codes of "fair" labor competition in these industries. In the textile code the Negro unskilled laborer is classified as a cleaner or outside worker, thereby being excluded from the minimum wage provisions. According to an article in the September issue of the magazine, "Opportunity," three million Negro workers (domestics, personal servants, farm laborers, unskilled workers, etc.) are excluded entirely from the N.R.A. codes. In the codes that provide a minimum wage for Negroes, the differential is from 25 per cent to 50 per cent less. In the lumber code there is a wide disparity in the rates of wages paid to the Northern white lumber workers and those paid to the Negro lumber workers of the South. Frances Perkins, Secretary of Labor, admitting the open discriminatory practices of the N.R.A. states: "The low rates of twenty-five cents and twenty-seven cents per hour for the two Southern districts are presumably based on the predominance of Negro labor in those districts." To overcome such flagrant disparity, she gives the solution that the Negro must have "increased wages that will not unfairly compete with the wages of white laborers." This is the common practice of the federal government amongst Negro workers of the Federal Barge Line, operated by the War Department. This strike in East St. Louis and St. Louis was against rotten working conditions of 12-15 hours per day, for which the men received pay for two hours' work. The N.R.A. Labor Board refused to give a hearing to the men; but the officials called the police who, through intimidation methods, tried to break the strike. During the application of the codes in the South, especially where there were wage increases, rather than give these increases to the Negro worker, the employer discharged him for the white worker.

The illusions in the "New Deal" among the Negro and white toilers were being shaken as the programme became a reality. Employment ceased; wages were cut; lay-offs set in; continued poverty and misery looked into the faces of the workers. Consequently there developed on the background of rapidly worsening conditions of the toilers a movement against the N.R.A. and its codes of "fair" competition for labor. This movement gained in momentum, as it swept every part of the country.

Naturally such wide disaffection took its sharpest form among the most exploited. To repel this deepening mass upsurge of Negro and white, which defied the dictates of the American Federation of Labor officialdom and the government to harness it, the State and the employers, throwing caution to the winds, but under a well-prepared barrage of demagogy, let loose sharp and intensified and repressive measures against the toilers.

The Negro masses felt the full strength of the hammer blows of the growing reaction of the N.R.A. They did not only receive wage-cuts and were thrown out of jobs, but were attacked on every front. Lynchings increased in number and savageness. Over forty were lynched during the first year of the N.R.A. The Blue Eagle, emblem of the N.R.A., in a new wave of lynchings set out to crush with flame and torch, rope and gun, every bit of militant resistance of the Negro masses. Lynchings, legal and extra-legal, received the sanction of employers and high State officials. They became holidays "in highly-cultured America" that recalled all the barbarous acts of the blackest days of the medieval period committed in the name of religion.

It was in this whipped-up lynch atmosphere that the lynch trials were set for the Scottsboro boys, and the legal lynching of Euel Lee took place. "Liberal" America, with Roosevelt at the helm of the "New Deal" ship, was determined to make the black man pay with his life for the misgivings of the N.R.A.

But the workers did not submit to this sharper terror easily. Under militant leadership, protests and struggles developed. The League of Struggle for Negro Rights issued a call for a nation-wide drive against lynchings and Negro oppression. The first united front regional conference against lynching was held in Baltimore, Maryland.

Baltimore is the home of the "liberal" democratic governor, Ritchie, an ardent supporter of the N.R.A. It is close to the Eastern shore where George Armwood was lynched and burned to a chair by the elite citizens. These same people threatened to lynch the attorney of the International Labor Defense, Bernard Ades, who very courageously defended Euel Lee. At the same time they asked to be allowed to supplant the courts, which in their opinion, were altogether too slow in legally lynching Lee. Ritchie openly stated that the mass resistance organized by the I.L.D., preventing the courts from rapidly carrying out the execution of Lee, was responsible for the mob heaping its hatred and vengeance in barbaric fashion on Armwood. Therefore "justice" must be served—Lee must hang by his neck—there can be no further stay or reprieve of the sentence.

It was in such a setting that the public hearing and investigation of lynchings and Negro oppression and the anti-lynch conference were called. The purpose of the public hearing and inquiry was: (1) to collect factual material and documentary evidence of the flagrant discriminatory practices against the Negroes; (2) to show the economic cause for the super-exploitation and oppression of the Negroes; (3) to assembly eye-witnesses to the Eastern shore lynchings and take their affidavits; (4) to receive investigators' reports on the new stages in the Scottsboro and Tuscaloosa cases; (5) to gather all of the available material and evidence to take before the President of the U.S.A. for the purpose of forcing the adoption of the Bill of Civil Rights presented to Congress by the Scottsboro marchers; (6) to publish from the collected material evidence a book similar to the Brown Book of the Hitler terror in Germany, with a similar title to "The Black Book of American Imperialism"; (7) to show the revolutionary way out.

The conference which immediately followed the hearing had its aim: (1) to launch a nation-wide drive against lynching under the leadership of the League of Struggle for Negro Rights and the International Labor Defense, building up the broadest kind of united front of joint actions; (2) to bring to the fore the programme of the L.S.N.R. in the struggle against national oppression; (3) to build the L.S.N.R. into a powerful mass organization; (4) to forge a mighty weapon out of the "Liberator" which should become the outspoken mouthpiece of the L.S.N.R. and the Negro people; (5) to show that only through revolutionary, only through the right of self-determination of the Negroes in the Black Belt could real freedom be achieved.

This immediate plan of action caused no little worry to the imperialists and their agents. They were aware of the deep dissatisfaction to the N.R.A. penetrating the Negro masses, especially discontent with the unequal wages established by the codes. They had before them the excellent response of the Negro class organizations. Therefore, these oppressors of the Negro people determined to defeat and sabotage the plan of action and attempt to smash the expanding influence of the Communist programme of liberation over the Negro people.

To accomplish such a slimy task, without creating consternation among the Negro people and white workers, the ruling class tried to proceed along concealed lines, using the "friends" of the Negroes to complete their deception. The arch supporter of Jim Crowism in Maryland and the hangman of Euel Lee, Governor Ritchie became the chief sponsor of a toothless anti-lynching Bill. Around the Governor and the Bill were grouped those betrayers of the struggles for Negro liberation, the National Association for the Advancement of Colored People and the Urban League; the white chauvinist apologists, the Socialist Party of Maryland. Previously the socialists had made a sham of asking that Ritchie should be impeached for his laxness in the Armwood lynching. But they withdrew from this position to support the lynchers of the Negro people. An attempt was made to draw the Negro masses into this false struggle. Extensive preparations were made to hold a mass meeting on the anti-lynching Bill to be presented to the Maryland legislature. After issuing thousands of leaflets, utilizing the press and pulpit, and conducting a campaign of shameful slander and lies against the L.S.N.R. and the I.L.D., the true defenders of the rights of Negro people, the meeting was held. But only 125 people responded to their frenzied efforts.

In contrast to this, the L.S.N.R. and the I.L.D., with considerable help from the Communist Party, mobilized the trade unions, certain locals of the A.F. of L., Negro organizations, unemployed organizations, and individuals for a united front and a minimum programme of action. At the same time the treacherous acts of the Negro misleaders and their white liberal friends were exposed. The response was good. The public inquiry in the New Albert Hall drew a capacity crowd of 2,000 paid admissions. To the conference over 700 delegates were elected from New York, New Jersey, Connecticut, Philadelphia, Baltimore, Washington, D.C. and the Eastern shore. Steel workers, dock workers, employed and unemployed, Negro and white, sincere intellectuals, professionals, members from the N.A.A.C.P. locals, Negro lodges and churches were delegates.

The revolutionary programme of the L.S.N.R., the struggle for equal rights of the Negroes in the North and for self-determination of the Negro majority in the Black Belt, was accepted as the only way to beat back the attacks of the white ruling class by the overwhelming majority of the delegates. The speeches of rank and file workers told of their willingness to join a fighting united front, rejecting the legal pussy-footing programme of the reformists. These workers gave the assurance of carrying the L.S.N.R. plan of action back to their organizations to help build up the drive against Negro oppression.

At the inquiry a large tribunal of judges, composed of workers, intellectuals and professionals was elected. Eyewitnesses from the Eastern shore spoke. Evidence was introduced by investigators from Tuscaloosa and Scottsboro cases. Before the eyes of an aroused working class and Negro people were unfolded the atrocities of American imperialism and its "New Deal" for the Negro masses. The indictment of the guilty for the long history of subjugation and humiliation, for the brutal oppression of a whole nation and for the new wave of lynching was thrust into the face of the white ruling class. The conference and the hearing threw out the challenge to mobilize mass resistance; to fight against Negro oppression.

Outstanding among the shortcomings were: (1) an underestimation of the tremendous response, in spite of poor preparations, to the hearing and the conference which called for revolutionary struggle against Negro persecution; (2) insufficient work done by the Communist workers, especially in the New York district, to penetrate A.F. of L. locals, working-class organizations and the new Negro organizations; (3) failure to answer the question of delegates concretely how they can work alone after returning home to carry out the fight against Negro oppression; (4) lack of preparations and popularizing of the *Liberator* and sale of the pamphlet containing the programme and manifesto of the L.S.N.R..

These mistakes must be corrected in the conferences which are to be held in Chicago, Cleveland, St. Louis, etc.

American imperialism and its new disguise, the "New Deal," the N.R.A., shall not go unchallenged in its grinding under its iron heel of oppression the Negro nation. It shall be met with stubborn resistance and working-class determination in battle, with mass mobilization of the Negro people and white workers, fighting for land, equality and freedom for a nation of 12,000,000 Negroes under the yoke of American imperialism.

A Betrayer of the Negro Liberation Struggle
By B.D. Amis
International Press Correspondence, June 29, 1934.

The present world crisis has brought untold misery and suffering to the peoples in the colonial, semi-colonial and capitalist countries. Starvation, scanty means of existence, increased terror and denial of elementary rights of mankind are the lot of millions of Negroes. But the capitalist class does not limit itself to terror alone, it also utilizes the method of penetrating the ranks of the working class with elements who have ideas which are alien and harmful to the cause of national liberation. Such ideas and an enemy have been discovered in the editorial board of the "Negro Board," the international Negro magazine.

George Padmore, in a small way, has taken his place alongside of the arch-betrayers of the Negro liberation struggle. Padmore has become a petty-bourgeois nationalist with connections with agent-provocateurs and enemies of the Negro liberation struggle.

Let us examine the path taken by Padmore. In a most feeble effort to justify his position and a profound lack of confidence in the revolutionary white workers, he claims: "What you white comrades have never understood and will never be able to understand is the psychology of the Negro."

Therefore, he gives the implication that the task of building up a united front, a wall of unity in struggle of Negro and white toilers against capitalism is impossible and the distrust of the Negroes in revolutionary white workers cannot be overcome, thus the gap between the Negro and white workers is being widened and the class enemy is allowed to utilize this division for its own ends. But this theory is enriched with his idea of saving Liberia. Liberia today stands in a position of a subject vassal State to the imperialists of the United States and England. The struggle of the Liberian natives for freedom is the struggle in the first place to drive out the American and British imperialists. But the white toilers of imperialist England, America and other countries, according to Padmore, are not interested in this struggle. He considers that Liberia is a free country, that American imperialism, through its agent, Firestone, does not occupy a dominant position and is not enslaving the native population. The main struggle today, in the words of Padmore, is to prevent "intervention and annexation" and to raise money for reform of the country. The struggle against slavery conditions on the rubber plantations of Firestone, the struggle for higher wages, the struggle for elementary democratic rights are excluded from the programmed of Padmore.

This is not a new theory. It has its origin in race theories, that the race is superior to the class. This theory means the perpetuation of the artificial barriers of white supremacy. Therefore, Negroes must unite to fight for their own interests as a race and against all whites.

The national liberation struggles of the millions of oppressed Negro peoples is closely linked up with the struggle of the white working class (the proletarian struggle) against capitalism. There cannot be any separation of the struggles of the white toilers for the betterment of their conditions from the struggles of oppressed Negro peoples. The unification of these struggles results in the powerful organization and concentration of working-class resistance to our enemy and hastens his downfall.

One of the means of increasing the profit of decaying capitalism and attempting to secure its tottering position is the establishment of trustified organizations of the type of Firestone Rubber Company. Such an agent of American capitalism has entered Liberia. Firestone robs the natives of their land, hires the same natives for starvation wages and in the most brutal manner exploits and oppresses the working population in order to produce a greater amount of raw material to be manufactured and thrown upon the market at the lowest possible price in order to undersell competitors.

At the same time Liberia finds itself in the economic crisis and is forced to take loans from the imperialist countries. These loans naturally subjugate Liberia to the creditor nation. Thus it is that American imperialism and its agents in Liberia are in a position to dictate their policy to this "free" State. To deny the role of American imperialism and at the same time to fail to see the struggle that is going on between England and America for the most dominant position in Liberia is attempting to cover up the enslavement and fierce terror against the native workers and help to continue the system of robbery and oppression. To spread such false ideas makes it more difficult to organize the struggle for complete freedom. But this is a deliberate policy of the white ruling class.

Can the freedom of the native workers be purchased by raising five million dollars or any other large sums? Does freedom come through such a utopian plan? Let us not forget Garvey, the father of such an idea, who introduced the "back to Africa movement" in the same manner. Only the lowest individual, trying to deceive honest toilers and further his own personal ambitions, would in the employ of our enemy oppressors, introduce the plan, called: "'Save Liberia Committee'—to raise five million dollars through donations to carry out internal reforms and national reconstruction"—without establishing the fundamental fact that these things can only be won through mass struggle. The struggle to abolish slavery (which exists in the real sense of the word) is a revolutionary struggle. As long as huge profits can be made from slave labor, as long as the higher strata of the native population can be bribed by the big corporations and landlords, it is childish to think that the imperialist bandits will give one concession without it being forced from them by the mass struggles of the toiling population. Reforms that will benefit the native toilers will come through revolutionary struggle. To speak of securing freedom in any other way is the same theory as put forward by the social democrats who have their counterpart in the Negro reformists. These people are against mass revolutionary struggle and are the main supports of the capitalist class, in helping to beat back the rising revolutionary movement.

Lastly, the fact is that Padmore not only has connection with the renegade elements of the Negro liberation movement and of the proletarian class struggle, but he has given information to the police about the developing Negro liberation struggle. When one stoops so low as to turn over the names and addresses of seamen, who are arrested, it shows where his class interests lie.

The blood of those who have been lynched, shot, tarred and feathered whipped at the post and cast into dark dungeons has not been shed in vain. This persecution of our fellow-toilers shall drive us onward to struggle more determinedly for complete emancipation. No betrayer can stop our progress. There is only one way out—the way of revolutionary struggle.

CHAPTER 8
THE CIO AND SWOC

Harrisburg State Capitol Of Jim Crow:
A Great Convention,
Delegates Smash Jim Crow Barriers

By B.D. Amis, Organizer S.W.O.C.
Labor Press, April 27, 1938.

The other day I had the good fortune to be in Harrisburg to attend the first State Convention of the C.I.O. Harrisburg is the State Capitol. The City is very beautiful; new capitol buildings are being erected; planned scenery; new highways; but of course our "Great Democratic Administration" has not yet come to the point of building on a mass scale decent homes for workers. It is too early.

But this beauty was almost nullified by the unwritten law generally practiced in the public institutions—of Jim Crow—no Negroes allowed. Of course there is a Civil Rights law on the statute books. But this law is toothless, consequently, who among big business pays any attention to it? You can't enforce it anyway.

Hash-house restaurants, greasy spoon joints, peanut Joes' taprooms and all other "respectable" places quietly tell all Negro customers, "sorry, we can't take care of you—you know how it is."

This was the situation which confronted our Steel delegates who, to say the least, were shocked. Our delegates from Philadelphia and surrounding territory, colored and white, all registered at the same hotel: all ate together; all attended the same places of amusement; wherever one went all went. When this was told to some of the more timid delegates and residents of the Capitol, they were amazed. They asked, "How did you get away with it?"

One Brother stated: "Well, we don't recognize color; we are all in the same lodge, we all work together and fight together and when we get ready to go anyplace, we all go together. If they don't treat our colored brothers the same as the white Brothers, we tell them "there's a 'New Deal'." The S.W.O.C. is in town—cut out that monkey business or if you don't—did you ever hear of boycott?"

He finished by stating: "The C.I.O. teaches us that only in unity is there strength and we will be able to better our conditions. We workers can't fight among ourselves."

Our Convention made history for the Trade Union movement. It was a great Democratic body of 1280 delegates with a goodly number of colored delegates coming from the U.M.W.A. and the E.W.O.C. The Convention struck a keynote of unity and showed quite clearly that its main objective was to keep intact the great Labor Movement of the State of Pennsylvania.

This Convention was made possible because 80 per cent of the unions represented had "committed the crime" of organizing the unorganized and had agreed to the policy of the C.I.O. and had attempted to keep intact the Penna. State Federation of Labor. This was stated by William Green as a reason for issuing the order of expulsion.

The Convention in a short period of time, produced a legislative program and a number of resolutions all of a progressive character. The resolution to support the Anti-Lynching Bill was unanimously adopted with the recommendation to all delegates to return to their respective local unions and have them send telegrams and postal cards to various members of Congress and the State Legislature, demanding that they throw their weight behind this bill for its passage. This was very encouraging and inspiring to all the delegates.

After the adjournment of the Convention, a number of us delegates— colored and white—walked into a very swanky restaurant and began to take seats. We noticed that there was a very hurried conference among the waitresses. After a couple of minutes, the waitresses came with water and menus in hand and asked what we would have. We noticed that each waitress had a large green button pinned on her apron on which was inscribed "Local No. __ of the A.F. of L."

One of the delegates, seeing the button, looked up at a waitress and asked, "what does that mean?"

She replied "A friend of [John L.] Lewis. If we were not, there possibly would have been some objection to the colored delegate."

To Labor A Challenge
By B.D. Amis, Representative S.W.O.C.
Non-Partisan News, May 7, 1938.

Rarely have the people (I mean the great mass of producers, not the coupon clippers) of this Commonwealth been called upon to decide emphatically what their voice in the State Government shall be. This question is to be determined on May 17th.

History has ordained that Labor must lead the march on to the road of the emancipation of the common people. But there are certain individuals (Democratic State Committee) who would ignore history, who would disregard the will and the demands of the majority of the people.

The question is, are we, the people, going to permit an autocratic minority to dictate to the majority? Are we to submit to government without direct representation? The answer must be no! A NO which will give Thomas Kennedy a decisive majority on May 17th.

The Democratic State Committee and its rulers have issued a challenge to Labor. They fear the power of a progressive mass Labor movement. Such a movement means support to President Roosevelt's program on economic security. It means a bludgeon blow to the reactionary forces in government which support the Fords, Girdlers, Weirs, Remington-Rands, etc. It means a pointing of the way to greater economic freedom.

These people would retard the progress of Labor. They attack the Wagner Labor Act, sufficient appropriation for the needs of the unemployed, housing program for workers, the anti-lynching bill, the O'Connell Peace Bill, wages and hours laws, and every bit of progressive labor legislation.

We are not going backwards. We must support New Deal legislation. We want still better legislation to do away with many inequalities. We want the liberty which will give all a decent living in accordance with the natural wealth of our country.

At present, our best guarantee is to rally the Labor Movement.

Labor Demonstrated Power in Primary Elections
By B.D. Amis, SWOC Representative
Labor Press, May 26, 1938.

Let no one tell you that the progressive labor movement in Pennsylvania suffered a defeat in the recent primaries. It is true that you hear from certain reactionary sections—National Republican Party leaders, Landon and Co.; the Tory Press; and a few misleaders of Labor—backslapping and crying aloud as in the *New York Times*, "C.I.O. defeated in Pennsylvania"; "C.I.O. is on the wane."

But these cries only reflect the alarm and fear existing in anti-Labor ranks. The alarm is over the demonstrated substantial gains of Labor to a new powerful position within the ranks of the New Deal. The fear is that a unified Labor Movement means certain defeat to the Republican Party and the reactionaries.

Thomas Kennedy polled over a half million votes, carrying the majority of the counties and was defeated by a scant 65,000 votes. This tremendous outpouring of voting strength came mainly, not from the middle class sections, but particularly where the Trade Union Movement was strongest and where there had been developed fairly functioning branches of Labor's Non-Partisan League, Kennedy Clubs and Progressive Democratic organizations for support of Kennedy.

The primary revealed to a large extent the role Labor is going to play in New Deal politics by the Democratic Party of the State. It showed the tremendous gains of the C.I.O. in steel and other industries. And above all, demonstrated the real power of Labor and what can be expected once the Labor Party is united.

Factors which prevented victory can be summed up as:

1. The split in the Trade Union movement; William Green's fight against the CIO and his instructions to all AF of L organizations to vote against Kennedy.

2. Margiotti, a third Democratic candidate, running as a Progressive.

3. Insufficient broad educational and propaganda campaign.

4. Lateness in establishing a greater number of Labor's non-Partisan League branches. Of course we need not mention that Labor did not have the political machine with which to corral votes, nor the money to pour into the campaign. Also, it cannot be forgotten that this was the first time that Labor as an independent political force, threw its cap into the arena and battled against the veterans of a well organized political machine.

A great and valuable experience was learned. Large sections of A.F. of L. workers ignored the instructions of William Green and voted for Kennedy. Outstanding for victory and political recognition of Labor is the urgent need for unity between the C.I.O. and the A.F. of L. Unity is essential to defeat the reactionaries and labor-hating employers, to defeat the Republican Party which is a spear head of attack against the New Deal legislation. And particularly is it urgent to safe-guard the Wagner Labor Act which is being attacked from all sides at the instigation of "Big Business."

The Democratic State Committee cannot expect Jones and Earle to carry the State Banner of the New Deal to victory over the outspoken treacherous, anti-labor Republican Party spokesmen—Grundy, Pew, Mellon, Jones and company, without having the full support and help from the powerful labor machinery during the primaries. There must be unity in the Democratic Party. Signs of this have already appeared in the statement of Governor Earle, "Welcoming all Back!" This is not sufficient. Labor must be recognized by the Democratic State Committee as a component part. It can't ignore in this crisis the 520,00 voters. This vote expressed the desire and the demand of the common people.

Labor is stronger than ever before. Its strength has been demonstrated. The cry must be louder than ever, "For a united Labor Movement," "For Unity among the Democratic forces."

We must keep the machinery which rallied a half million voters as a means of securing our newly won positions in the political field. Not only that, but the branches of Labor's Non-Partisan League must be extended and must become the nerve centers in the field of politics to educate larger masses of workers, progressives and liberals and to prepare them to give stubborn resistance to defeat all who are against the President's economic security program—to defeat reaction—to defeat those who support the war makers and the American brand of fascism.

The Pennsylvania Labor Movement stands as a bulwark of strength uniting all forces for economic security, peace and progress. A Pennsylvania Labor Movement united along progressive lines, spells "Happy Days" to the workers and is their best guarantee for an effective minimum wage and hour law. It is protection against wage cuts and a return to the old conditions.

It lies within the power of Labor to achieve this unity by forcing the labor splitters to accede to our demands. Labor's ability has been demonstrated. We need now to cash in on our power.

Telegram, May 27, 1938.

B.D Amis. Rep Steel Workers Organizing Committee. Lorraine Hotel. An Answer Postal Telegraph 23TD. Answering your recent communication concerning amendment to United States Housing Act. Be assured I am in sympathy with the amendment. The matter is in the hands of the democratic leaders.

James J. Davis, US Senator.

Appeal to Workers of Atlantic Steel
By B.D. Amis, SWOC Representative
Labor Press, June 2, 1938.

Never before was the need of organization as great in your plant as it is today. Business conditions are getting worse, lay-offs are increasing and those fortunate enough to work part-time are threatened with wage cuts.

Naturally, under such circumstances, your employer is not going to encourage you to join an organization which will protect you from the ravages of bad business. But on the contrary, he will place every obstacle in your path and will poison your mind about the union. This may be done directly or indirectly. But the results are the same. You are the sufferer. You remain a slave of your employer.

How the Employer Works

To the colored worker, the anti-union employer is very kind and humane. Rather than give you real wages which compare with union standards, he will give you a smile, a pat on the back, a suit of clothes, a bag of potatoes; or he may have you clean his car, go to his home to clean his yard or wash windows for the Mrs.

He is a good boss. At Christmas time he gives you a chicken. And if you get in jail, he will get you out and you will take all of the 50 years to repay him for his kindness. Thus, to you he is an ideal person, a real Christian.

To the foreign-born worker, this same boss acts in a similar manner. The foreign-born worker, who knows little of American laws and customs, unfortunately, may get into trouble. The boss readily gets him out. The worker has left his family in the "old country" and feeling lonely, wants them to join him. The "big-hearted" boss lends John the money and John sends for his family. But John works the rest of his natural days to pay back this debt of gratitude.

But the results of all this "kind-heartedness" on the part of your "gracious" employer prevents the worker from getting real wages and keeps him chained to his boss. You are afraid to join a union. Why? Because you'll lose your job. You are afraid to attend a union meeting. Why? Because the boss may have some one there who will see you and report about your presence at such a meeting.

BRIEF EPILOGUE

During the Nazi-Soviet Pact period (August 1939 to Jun 22, 1941), Amis and American Communists adopted the position that the U.S. should stay out of World War II.

Scorns Defense Committee Post; Cites Oppression of Negroes

[Pittsburgh Courier, March 29, 1941.]

PHILADELPHIA, March 27. Declaring his disinterest in giving support to imperialistic nations whether they be British, Nazi or Fascist, B. DeWayne Amis, secretary-treasurer of the Catering Industry Employees Union No. 758, 507 S. 16th St, demanded that his name be withdrawn immediately as one of the members of the Committee to Defend America by Aiding the Allies.

The demand was made this week in a letter addressed to Conyers Read, chairman of the committee. Its full text, as released by Mr. Amis, follows:

Mr. Conyers Read,
Chairman of Committee
To Defend America
North American Bldg.
Philadelphia, Pa.

Dear Mr. Reid:

I am in receipt of your letter of March 18 which includes my name as one of the members of the Committee to Defend America by Aiding the Allies, I am requesting that you immediately withdraw my name from this committee as it has been used without authorization, and that I am not interested in giving my support to the battles of the various imperialistic nations, whether they be British, Nazi or Fascist.

There may be different shades in the character of these nations, but when it comes to oppressing my people and giving them nationhood and democratic rights, they are all cut from the same cloth.

My sympathies are with the oppressed and super exploited African and Indian Colonials, the Irish people and others who suffer under this yoke.

My people as a whole, do not want to have anything to do with those nations who refuse to give freedom to the Black man, and I am convinced that the fight we should be waging should be a fight for the democratic rights of the Negroes in America (abolition of lynching, jim-crowism, poll-tax), liquidation of unemployment, placing these workers in useful service, building decent homes for workers and, in general, the raising of their living standards. I trust that this statement shall definitely clarify this matter.

(Signed)

B. DeWAYNE AMIS

After the German invasion of the Soviet Union in June 1941, Stalin became an official ally of the U.S. and American Communists strenuously supported the war effort. During the early cold war, McCarthyism virtually destroyed the American Communist movement. Like most radicals in these years, Amis turned in a new direction, although he never departed from his egalitarian principles. He became a family man who resided in Philadelphia, Pennsylvania. He subsequently worked for the Gulf Oil Company where he continued his union activities. Moreover, he did all that he could in those years to protect his children from the anticommunist wrath of McCarthyism and harassment by the FBI. As a retired and aging radical activist, he watched the unfolding of the civil rights and peace movements of the 1960s and had the satisfaction of seeing several of his children carry on the struggle in their own manner. However, he left the actual field work to younger colleagues as he cheered from the sidelines. He lived out the last decades of his life in a conservative America in the seventies and eighties, and died on June 9, 1993 in Alexandria, Virginia.

APPENDIX

I. The 1928 Comintern Resolution on the Negro
Question in the United States

1. The industrialization of the South, the concentration of a new Negro working class population in the big cities of the East and North and the entrance of the Negroes into the basic industries on a mass scale, create the possibility for the Negro workers, under the leadership of the Communist Party, to assume the hegemony of all Negro liberation movements, and to increase their importance and role in the revolutionary struggle of the American proletariat.

The Negro working class has reached a stage of development which enables it, if properly organized and well led, to fulfill successfully its double historical mission:

(a) To play a considerable role in the class struggle against American imperialism as an important part of the American working class; and

(b) To lead the movement of the oppressed masses of the Negro population.

2. The bulk of the Negro population (86%) live in the southern states; of this number 74 per cent live in the rural districts and are dependent almost exclusively upon agriculture for a livelihood. Approximately one-half of these rural dwellers live in the so-called "Black Belt," in which area they constitute more than 50 per cent of the entire population. The great mass of the Negro agrarian population are subject to the most ruthless exploitation and persecution of a semi-slave character. In addition to the ordinary forms of capitalist exploitation, American imperialism utilizes every possible form of slave exploitation (peonage, share-cropping, landlord supervision of crops and marketing, etc.) for the purpose of extracting super-profits. On the basis of these slave remnants, there has grown up a super-structure of social and

political inequality that expresses itself in Lynching, segregation, Jim Crowism, etc.

Necessary Conditions for National Revolutionary Movement.

3. The various forms of oppression of the Negro masses, who are concentrated mainly in the so-called "Black Belt," provide the necessary conditions for a national revolutionary movement among the Negroes. The Negro agricultural laborers and the tenant farmers feel most the pressure of white persecution and exploitation. Thus, the agrarian problem lies at the root of the Negro national movement. The great majority of Negroes in the rural districts of the South are not "reserves of capitalist reaction," but potential allies of the revolutionary proletariat. Their objective position facilitates their transformation into a revolutionary force, which, under the leadership of the proletariat, will be able to participate in the joint struggle with all other workers against capitalist exploitation.

4. It is the duty of the Negro workers to organize through the mobilization of the broad masses of the Negro population the struggle of the agricultural laborers and tenant farmers against all forms of semi-feudal oppression. On the other hand, it is the duty of the Communist Party of the U.S.A. to mobilize and rally the broad masses of the white workers for active participation in this struggle. For that reason the Party must consider the beginning of systematic work in the South as one of its main tasks, having regard for the fact that the bringing together of the workers and toiling masses of all nationalities for a joint struggle against the landowners and the bourgeoisie is one of the most important aims of the Communist International, as laid down in the resolutions on the national and colonial question of the Second and Sixth Congresses of the Comintern.

For Complete Emancipation of Oppressed Negro Race

5. To accomplish this task, the Communist Party must come out as the champion of the right of the oppressed Negro race for full emancipation. While continuing and intensifying the struggle under the slogan of full social and political equality for the Negroes, which must remain the central slogan of our Party for work among the masses, the Party must come out openly and unreservedly for the right of the Negroes to national self-determination in the southern states, where the Negroes form a majority of the population. The struggle for equal rights and the propaganda for the slogan of self-

determination must be linked up with the economic demands of the Negro masses, especially those directed against the slave remnants and all forms of national and racial oppression. Special stress must be laid upon organizing active resistance against Lynching, Jim Crowism, segregation and all other forms of oppression of the Negro population.

6. All work among the Negroes, as well as the struggle for the Negro cause among the whites, must be used, based upon the changes which have taken place in the relationship of classes among the Negro population. The existence of a Negro industrial proletariat of almost two million workers makes it imperative that the main emphasis should be placed on these new proletarian forces. The Negro workers must be organized under the leadership of the Communist Party, and thrown into joint struggle together with the white workers. The Party must learn to combine all demands of the Negroes with the economic and political struggle of the workers and the poor farmers.

American Negro Question Part of World Problem

7. The Negro question in the United States must be treated in its relation to the Negro questions and struggles in other parts of the world. The Negro race everywhere is an oppressed race. Whether it is a minority (U.S.A., etc.), majority (South Africa) or inhabits a so-called independent state (Liberia, etc.), the Negroes are oppressed by imperialism. Thus, a common tie of interest is established for the revolutionary struggle of race and national liberation from imperialist domination of the Negroes in various parts of the world. A strong Negro revolutionary movement in the U.S.A. will be able to influence and direct the revolutionary movement in all those parts of the world where the Negroes are oppressed by imperialism.

8. The proletarianization of the Negro masses makes the trade unions the principal form of mass organization. It is the primary task of the Party to play an active part and lead in the work of organizing the Negro workers and agricultural laborers in trade unions. Owing to the refusal of the majority of the white unions in the U.S.A., led by the reactionary leaders, to admit Negroes to membership, steps must be immediately taken to set up special unions for those Negro workers who are not allowed to join the white unions. At the same time, however, the struggles for the inclusion of Negro workers in the existing unions must be intensified and concentrated upon, special attention must be given to those unions in which the statutes and rules set up special limitations against the admission of Negro workers. Primary duty of Communist Party in this connection is to wage a merciless struggle against the A. F. of L. bureaucracy, which prevents the Negro workers from joining the white workers' unions. The organization of special trade unions for the Negro masses must be carried out as part and parcel of the struggle against

the restrictions imposed upon the Negro workers and for their admission to
the white workers' unions. The creation of separate Negro unions should in
no way weaken the struggle in the old unions for the admission of Negroes
on equal terms. Every effort must be made to see that all the new unions organized by the Left wing and by the Communist Party should embrace the
workers of all nationalities and of all races. The principle of one union for all
workers in each industry, white and black, should cease to be a mere slogan
of propaganda, and must become a slogan of action.

Party Trade Union Work Among Negroes

9. While organizing the Negroes into unions and conducting an aggressive struggle against the anti-Negro trade union policy of the A. F. of L., the
Party must pay more attention than it has hitherto done to the work in the
Negro workers' organizations, such as the Brotherhood of Sleeping Car Porters, Chicago Asphalt Workers' Union, and so on. The existence of two million Negro workers and the further industrialization of the Negroes demand a
radical change in the work of the Party among the Negroes. The creation of
working class organizations and the extension of our influence in the existing working class Negro organizations, are of much greater importance than
the work in bourgeois and petty-bourgeois organizations, such as the National Association for the Advancement of Colored People, the Pan-African
Congress, etc.

10. The American Negro Labor Congress continues to exist only nomi-
nally. Every effort should be made to strengthen this organization as a me-
dium through which we can extend the work of the Party among the Negro
masses and mobilize the Negro workers under our leadership. After careful
preparatory work, which must be started at once, another convention of the
American Negro Labor Congress should be held. A concrete plan must also
be presented to the Congress for an intensified struggle for the economic,
social, political and national demands of the Negro masses. The program of
the American Negro Labor Congress must deal specially with the agrarian
demands of the Negro farmers and tenants in the South.

11. The importance of trade union work imposes special tasks upon the
Trade Union Educational League. The T.U.E.L. has completely neglected
the work among the Negro workers, notwithstanding the fact that these
workers are objectively in a position to play a very great part in carrying
through the program of organizing the unorganized. The closest contact must
be established between the T.U.E.L. and the Negro masses. The T.U.E.L.
must become the champion in the struggle for the rights of the Negroes in
the old unions, and in the organizing of new unions for both Negroes and
whites, as well as separate Negro unions.

White Chauvinism Evidenced in the American Party

The C.E.C. of the American Communist Party itself stated in its resolution of April 30, 1928, that "the Party as a whole has not sufficiently realized the significance of work among the Negroes." Such an attitude toward the Party work among the Negroes is, however, not satisfactory. The time is ripe to begin within the Party a courageous campaign of self-criticism concerning the work among the Negroes. Penetrating self-criticism is the necessary preliminary condition for directing the Negro work along new lines.

13. The Party must bear in mind that white chauvinism, which is the expression of the ideological influence of American imperialism among the workers, not only prevails among different strata of the white workers in the U.S.A., but is even reflected in various forms in the Party itself. White chauvinism has manifested itself even in open antagonism of some comrades to the Negro comrades. In some instances where Communists were called upon to champion and to lead in the most vigorous manner the fight against white chauvinism, they instead yielded to it. In Gary, white members of the Workers Party protested against Negroes eating in the restaurant controlled by the Party. In Detroit, Party members, yielding to pressure, drove out Negro comrades from a social given in aid of the miners on strike.

Whilst the Party has taken certain measures against these manifestations of white chauvinism, nevertheless those manifestations must be regarded as indications of race prejudice even in the ranks of the Party, which must be fought with the utmost energy.

14. An aggressive fight against all forms of white chauvinism must be accompanied by a widespread and thorough educational campaign in the spirit of internationalism within the Party, utilizing for this purpose to the fullest possible extent the Party schools, the Party press and the public platform, to stamp out all forms of antagonism, or even indifference among our white comrades toward the Negro work. This educational work should be conducted simultaneously with a campaign to draw the white workers and the poor farmers into the struggle for the support of the demands of the Negro workers.

Tasks of Party in Relation to Negro Work

15. The Communist Party of the U.S.A. in its treatment of the Negro question must all the time bear in mind this twofold task:

(a) To fight for the full rights of the oppressed Negroes and for their right to self-determination and against all forms of chauvinism, especially among the workers of the oppressing nationality.

(b) The propaganda and the day-to-day practice of international class solidarity must be considered as one of the basic tasks of the American Communist Party. The fight—by propaganda and by deeds—should be directed first and foremost against the chauvinism of the workers of the oppressing nationality as well as against bourgeois segregation tendencies of the oppressed nationality. The propaganda of international class solidarity is the necessary prerequisite for the unity of the working class in the struggle.

"The center of gravity in educating the workers of the oppressing countries in the principles of internationalism must inevitably consist in the propaganda and defense by these workers of the right of segregation by the oppressed countries. We have the right and duty to treat every socialist of an oppressing nation, who does not conduct such propaganda, as an imperialist and as a scoundrel." (Lenin, selected articles on the national question.)

16. The Party must seriously take up the task of training a cadre of Negro comrades as leaders, bring them into the Party schools in the U.S.A. and abroad, and make every effort to draw Negro proletarians into active and leading work in the Party, not confining the activities of the Negro comrades exclusively to the work among Negroes. Simultaneously, white workers must specially be trained for work among the Negroes.

17. Efforts must be made to transform the "Negro Champion" into a weekly mass organ of the Negro proletariat and tenant farmers. Every encouragement and inducement must be given to the Negro comrades to utilize the Party press generally.

Negro Work Part of General Work of Party

18. The Party must link up the struggle on behalf of the Negroes with the general campaigns of the Party. The Negro problem must be part and parcel of all and every campaign conducted by the Party. In the election campaigns, trade union work, the campaigns for the organization of the unorganized, anti-imperialist work, labor party campaign, International Labor Defense, etc., the Central Executive Committee must work out plans designed to draw the Negroes into active participation in all these campaigns, and at the same time to bring the white workers into the struggle on behalf of the Negroes' demands. It must be borne in mind that the Negro masses will not be won for the revolutionary struggles until such time as the most conscious section of the white workers show, by action, that they are fighting with the Negroes against all racial discrimination and persecution. Every

member of the Party must bear in mind that "the age-long oppression of the colonial and weak nationalities by the imperialist powers, has given rise to a feeling of bitterness among the masses of the enslaved countries as well as a feeling of distrust toward the oppressing nations in general and toward the proletariat of those nations."

19. The Negro women in industry and on the farms constitute a powerful potential force in the struggle for Negro emancipation. By reason of being unorganized to an even greater extent than male Negro workers, they are the most exploited section. The A. F. of L. bureaucracy naturally exercises toward them a double hostility, by reason of both their color and sex. It therefore becomes an important task of the Party to bring the Negro women into the economic and political struggle.

20. Only by an active and strenuous fight on the part of the white workers against all forms of oppression directed against the Negroes, will the Party be able to draw into its ranks the most active and conscious Negro workers —men and women—and to increase its influence in those intermediary organizations which are necessary for the mobilization of the Negro masses in the struggle against segregation, lynching, Jim Crowism, etc.

21. In the present struggle in the mining industry, the Negro workers participate actively and in large numbers. The leading role the Party played in this struggle has helped greatly to increase its prestige. Nevertheless, the special efforts being made by the Party in the work among the Negro strikers cannot be considered as adequate. The Party did not send enough Negro organizers into the coalfields, and it did not sufficiently attempt, in the first stages of the fight, to develop the most able Negro strikers and to place them in leading positions. The Party must be especially criticized for its failure to put Negro workers on the Presidium of the Pittsburgh Miners' Conference, doing so only after such representation was demanded by the Negroes themselves.

22. In the work among the Negroes, special attention should be paid to the role played by the churches and preachers who are acting on behalf of American imperialism. The Party must conduct a continuous and carefully worked out campaign among the Negro masses, sharpened primarily against the preachers and the churchmen, who are the agents of the oppressors of the Negro race.

Party Work Among Negro Proletariat and Peasantry

23. The Party must apply united front tactics for specific demands to the existing Negro petty bourgeois organizations. The purpose of these united front tactics should be the mobilizing of the Negro masses under the leadership of the Party, and to expose the treacherous petty bourgeois leadership of those organizations.

24. The Negro Miners Relief Committee and the Harlem Tenants League are examples of joint organizations of action which may serve as a means of drawing the Negro masses into struggle. In every case the utmost effort must be made to combine the struggle of the Negro workers with the struggle of the white workers, and to draw the white workers' organizations into such joint campaigns.

25. In order to reach the bulk of the Negro masses, special attention should be paid to the work among the Negroes in the South. For that purpose, the Party should establish a district organization in the most suitable locality in the South. Whilst continuing trade union work among the Negro workers and the agricultural laborers, special organizations of tenant farmers must be set up. Special efforts must also be made to secure the support of the share croppers in the creation of such organizations. The Party must undertake the task of working out a definite program of immediate demands, directed against all slave remnants, which will serve as the rallying slogans for the formation of such peasant organizations.

Henceforth the Workers (Communist) Party must consider the struggle on behalf of the Negro masses, the task of organizing the Negro workers and peasants and the drawing of these oppressed masses into the proletarian revolutionary struggle, as one of its major tasks, remembering, in the words of the Second Congress resolution, that "the victory over capitalism cannot be fully achieved and carried to its ultimate goal unless the proletariat and the toiling masses of all nations of the world rally of their own accord in a concordant and close union."

II. The 1930 Comintern Resolution on the Negro
Question in the United States

The C.P. of the United States has always acted openly and energetically against Negro oppression, and has thereby won increasing sympathy among the Negro population. In its own ranks, too, the Party has relentlessly fought the slightest evidences of white chauvinism, and has purged itself of the gross opportunism of the Lovestoneites. According to the assertions of these people, the "industrial revolution" will sweep away the remnants of slavery in the agricultural South, and will proletarianise the Negro peasantry, so that the Negro question, as a special national question, would thereby be presumably solved, or could be put off until the time of the socialist revolution in America. But the Party has not yet succeeded in overcoming in its own ranks all under-estimation of the struggle for the slogan of the right of self-determination, and still less succeeded in doing away with all *lack of clarity* on the Negro question. In the Party discussion the question was often wrongly put and much erroneous counter-poising of phases of the question occurred, thus, for instance, should the slogan of social equality or the slogan of the right of self-determination of the Negroes be emphasized. Should only propaganda for the Negroes' right to self-determination be carried on, or should this slogan be considered as a slogan of action; should separatist tendencies among the Negroes be supported or opposed; is the Southern region, thickly populated by Negroes, to be looked upon as a colony, or as an "integral part of the national economy of the United States," where presumably a revolutionary situation cannot arise independent of the general revolutionary development in the United States?

In the interest of the utmost clarity of ideas on this question the Negro question in the United States must be viewed from the standpoint of its peculiarity, namely as the question of an *oppressed nation*, which is in a peculiar and extraordinarily distressing situation of national oppression not only in view of the prominent *racial distinctions* (marked difference in the colour of skin, etc.), but above all because of considerable *social antagonism* (remnants of slavery). This introduces into the American Negro question an important, *peculiar* trait which is absent from the national question of other oppressed peoples. Furthermore, it is necessary to face clearly the inevitable distinction between the position of the Negro in the *South* and in the *North*, owing to the fact that at least three-fourths of the entire Negro population of the United States (12 million) live in compact masses in the South, most of them being peasants and agricultural labourers in a state of semi-serfdom, settled in the "Black Belt" and constituting the majority of the population, whereas the Negroes in the Northern States are for the most part industrial workers of the lowest categories who have recently come to the various industrial centres from the South (having often even fled from there).

The struggle of the Communists for the equal rights of the Negroes applies to all Negroes, in the North as well as in the South. The struggle for this slogan embraces all or almost all of the important special interests of the Negroes in the North, but not in the South, where the main Communist slo-

gan must be: *The right of self-determination of the Negroes in the Black Belt.*
These two slogans, however, are most closely connected. The Negroes in the
North are very much interested in winning the right of self-determination for
the Negro population of the Black Belt and can thereby hope for strong support for the establishment of true equality of the Negroes in the North. In the
South the Negroes are suffering no less but still more than in the North from
the glaring lack of all equality; for the most part the struggle for their most
urgent partial demands in the Black Belt is nothing more than the struggle
for their equal rights, and only the fulfillment of their main slogan, the right
of self-determination in the Black Belt, can assure them of true equality.

The Struggle for the Equal Rights of the Negroes

2. [*there is no item 1.*] The basis for the demand of equality of the Negroes is provided by the special yoke to which the Negroes in the United
States are subjected by the ruling classes. In comparison with the situation of
the other various nationalities and faces oppressed by American imperialism,
the yoke of the Negroes in the United States is of a peculiar nature and particularly oppressive. This is partly due to the historical past of the American
Negroes as imported slaves, but is much more due to the still existing slavery
of the American Negro which is immediately apparent, for example, in com-
paring their situation even with the situation of the Chinese and Japanese
workers in the West of the United States, or with the lot of the Philippinos
(Malay race) who are under colonial repression.

It is only a Yankee bourgeois lie to say that the yoke of Negro slavery
has been lifted in the United States. Formally it has been abolished, but in
practice the great majority of the Negro masses in the South are living in
slavery in the literal sense of the word. Formally, they are "free" as "tenant
farmers" or "contract labourers" on the big plantations of the white landowners, but actually, they are completely in the power of their exploiters;
they are not permitted, or else it is made impossible for them to leave their
exploiters; if they do leave the plantations, they are brought back and in
many cases whipped; many of them are simply taken prisoner under various
pretexts and, bound together with long chains, they have to do compulsory
labour on the roads. All through the South, the Negroes are not only deprived of all rights, and subjected to the arbitrary will of the white exploiters,
but they are also socially ostracized, that is, they are treated in general not as
human beings, but as cattle. But this ostracism regarding Negroes is not limited to the South. Not only in the South but throughout the United States, the
lynching of Negroes is permitted to go unpunished. Everywhere the American bourgeoisie surrounds the Negroes with an atmosphere of social ostracism.

The 100 per cent Yankee arrogance divides the American population into a series of castes, among which the Negroes constitute, so to speak, the caste of the "untouchables," who are in a still lower category than the lowest categories of human society, the immigrant labourers, the yellow immigrants and the Indians. In all big cities the Negroes have to live in special segregated ghettoes (and, of course, have to pay extremely high rent). In practice, marriage between Negroes and whites is prohibited, and in the South this is even forbidden by law. In various other ways, the Negroes are segregated, and if they overstep the bounds of the segregation they immediately run the risk of being ill-treated by the 100 per cent bandits. As wage-earners, the Negroes are forced to perform the lowest and most difficult work; they generally receive lower wages than the white workers and don't always get the same wages as white workers doing similar work, and their treatment is the very worst. Many A. F. of L. trade unions do not admit Negro workers in their ranks, and a number have organised special trade unions for Negroes so that they will not have to let them into their "good white society."

This whole system of "segregation" and "Jim Crowism" is a special form of national and social oppression under which the American Negroes have much to suffer. The origin of all this is not difficult to find: this Yankee arrogance towards the Negroes stinks of the disgusting atmosphere of the old slave market. This is downright robbery and slave-whipping barbarism at the peak of capitalist "culture."

3. The demand for equal rights in our sense of the word means not only demanding the same rights for the Negroes as the whites have in the United States at the present time but also demanding that the Negroes should be granted all rights and other advantages which we demand for the corresponding oppressed classes of whites (workers and other toilers). Thus in our sense of the word, the demand for equal rights means a continuous work of abolishment of all forms of economic and political oppression of the Negroes, as well as their social exclusion, the insults perpetrated against them and their segregation. This is to be obtained by constant struggle by the white and black workers for effective legal protection for the Negroes in all fields, as well as actual enforcement of their equality and combating of every expression of Negrophobia. One of the first Communist slogans is: Death for Negro lynching!

The struggle for the equal rights of the Negroes does not in any way exclude recognition and support for the Negroes' rights to their own special schools, government organs, etc., wherever the Negro masses put forward such national demands of their own accord. This will, however, in all probability occur to any great extent only in the Black Belt. In other parts of the country, the Negroes suffer above all from being shut out from the general social institutions and not from being prohibited to set up their own national institutions. With the development of the Negro intellectuals (principally in the "free" professions) and of a thin layer of small capitalist business people, there have appeared lately, not only definite efforts for developing a purely national Negro culture but also outspoken bourgeois tendencies towards Negro nationalism. The broad masses of the Negro population in the big industrial centres of the North are, however, making no efforts whatsoever to maintain and cultivate a national aloofness, they are, on the contrary, working for assimilation. This effort of the Negro masses can do much in the future to facilitate the progressive process of amalgamating the whites and Negroes into one nation, and it is under no circumstances the task of the Communists to give support to bourgeois nationalism in its fight with the progressive assimilation tendencies of the Negro working masses.

4. The slogan of equal rights of the Negroes *without a relentless struggle in practice against all manifestations of Negrophobia on the part of the American bourgeoisie* can be nothing but a deceptive liberal gesture of a sly slave-owner or his agent. This slogan is in fact repeated by "socialist" and many other bourgeois politicians and philanthropists who want to get publicity for themselves by appealing to the "sense of justice" of the American bourgeoisie in the individual treatment of the Negroes, and thereby sidetrack attention from the one effective struggle against the shameful system of "white superiority": from the *class struggle against the American bourgeoisie.* The struggle for equal rights for the Negroes is in fact, one of the most important parts of the proletarian class struggle of the United States.

The struggle for the equal rights for the Negroes must certainly take the form of common struggle by the white and black workers.

The increasing unity of the various working-class elements provokes constant attempts on the part of the American bourgeoisie to play one group against another, particularly the white workers against the black and the black workers against the immigrant workers and vice versa, and thus to promote divisions within the working-class, which contributes to the bolstering up of American capitalist rule. The Party must carry on a ruthless struggle against all these attempts of the bourgeoisie and do everything to strengthen the bonds of class solidarity of the working-class upon a lasting basis.

In the struggle for equal rights for the Negroes, however, it is the duty of the *white* workers to march at *the head* on this struggle. They must everywhere make a breach in the walls of segregation and "Jim Crowism" which have been set up by bourgeois slave-market morality. They must most ruthlessly unmask and condemn the hypocritical reformists and bourgeois "friends of Negroes" who, in reality, are only interested in strengthening the power of the enemies of the Negroes. They, the white workers, must boldly jump at the throat of the 100 per cent bandits who strike a Negro in the face. This struggle will be the test of the real international solidarity of the American white workers.

It is the special duty of the revolutionary Negro workers to carry on tireless activity among the Negro working masses to free them of their distrust of the white proletariat and draw them into the common front of the revolutionary class struggle against the bourgeoisie. They must emphasize with all force that the first rule of proletarian morality is that no worker who wants to be an equal member of his class must ever serve as a strike-breaker or a supporter of bourgeois politics. They must ruthlessly unmask all Negro politicians corrupted or directly bribed by American bourgeois ideology, who systematically interfere with the real proletarian struggle for the equal rights for the Negroes.

Furthermore, the Communist Party must resist all tendencies within its own ranks to ignore the Negro question as a national question in the United States, not only in the South, but also in the North. It is advisable for the Communist Party in the North to abstain from the establishment of any special Negro organisations, and in place of this to bring the black and white workers together in common organisations of struggle and joint action. Effective steps must be taken for the organisation of Negro workers in the T.U.U.L. and revolutionary trade unions. Under-estimation of this work takes various forms: lack of energy in recruiting Negro workers, in keeping them in our ranks and in drawing them into the full life of the trade unions, in selecting, educating and promoting Negro forces to leading functions in the organisation. The Party must make itself entirely responsible for the carrying through of this very important work. It is most urgently necessary to publish a popular mass paper dealing with the Negro question, edited by white and black comrades, and to have all active followers of this paper grouped organisationally.

The Struggle for the Right of Self-determination of the Negroes in the Black Belt

5. It is not correct to consider the Negro zone of the South as a colony of the United States. Such a characterisation of the Black Belt could be based in some respects only upon artificially construed analogies, and would create superfluous difficulties for the clarification of ideas. In rejecting this estimation, however, it should not be overlooked that it would be none the less false to try to make a fundamental distinction between the character of na-

tional oppression to which the colonial peoples are subjected and the yoke of other oppressed nations. Fundamentally, national oppression in both cases is of the same character, and is in the Black Belt in many respects worse than in a number of actual colonies. On the one hand the Black Belt is not in itself, either economically or politically, such a united whole as to warrant its being called a special colony of the United States, but on the other hand this zone is not, either economically or politically, such an, integral part of the whole United States as any other part of the country. Industrialisation in the Black Belt is not, as is generally the case in colonies properly speaking, in contradiction with the ruling interests of the imperialist bourgeoisie, which has in its hands the monopoly of the entire industry, but in so far as industry is developed here, it will in no way bring a solution to the question of living conditions of the oppressed Negro majority, or to the agrarian question, which lies at the basis of the national question. On the contrary, this question is still further aggravated as a result of the increase of the contradictions arising from the pre-capitalist forms of exploitation of the Negro peasantry and of a considerable portion of the Negro proletariat (miners, forestry workers, etc.) in the Black Belt, and at the same time owing to the industrial development here, the growth of the most important driving force of the national revolution, the black working-class, is especially strengthened. Thus, the prospect for the future is not an inevitable dying away of the national revolutionary Negro movement in the South, as Lovestone prophesied, but on the contrary, a great advance of this movement and the rapid approach of a revolutionary crisis in the Black Belt.

6. Owing to the peculiar situation in the Black Belt (the fact that the majority of the resident Negro population are farmers and agricultural labourers and that the capitalist economic system as well as political class rule there is not only of a special kind, but to a great extent still has pre-capitalist and semi-colonial features), the right of self-determination of the Negroes as the main slogan of the Communist Party in the Black Belt is appropriate. This, however, does not in any way mean that the struggle for equal rights of the Negroes in the Black Belt is less necessary or less well founded than it is in the North. On the contrary, here, owing to the whole situation, this struggle is even better founded, but the form of this slogan does not sufficiently correspond with the concrete requirements of the liberation struggle of the Negro population. Anyway, it is clear that in most cases it is a question of the daily conflicts of interest between the Negroes and the white rulers in the Black Belt on the subject of infringement of the most elementary equality rights of the Negroes by the whites. Daily events of the kind are: all Negro persecutions, all arbitrary economic acts of robbery by the white exploiters ("Black Man's Burden") and the whole system of so-called "Jim Crowism." Here, however, it is very important in connection with all these concrete cases of conflict to concentrate the attention of the Negro masses not so

much to the general demands of mere equality, but much more to some of the revolutionary basic demands arising from the concrete situation.

The slogan of the right of self-determination occupies the central place in the liberation struggle of the Negro population in the Black Belt against the yoke of American imperialism, but this slogan, as we see it, must be carried out only in connection with two other basic demands. Thus, there are three basic demands to be kept in mind in the Black Belt, namely, the following:

(1) *Confiscation of the landed property of the white landowners and capitalists for the benefit of the Negro farmers.* The landed property in the hands of the white American exploiters constitutes the most important material basis of the entire system of national oppression and serfdom of the Negroes in the Black Belt. More than three-quarters of all Negro farmers here are bound in actual serfdom to the farms and plantations of the white exploiters by the feudal system of "share cropping." Only on paper and not in practice are they freed from the yoke of their former slavery. The same holds completely true for the great mass of black contract labourers; here the contract is only the capitalist expression of the chains of the old slavery, which even to-day are not infrequently applied in their natural iron form on the roads of the Black Belt (chain-gang work). These are the main forms of present Negro slavery in the Black Belt and no breaking of the chains of this slavery is possible without confiscating all the landed property of the white masters. Without this revolutionary measure, without the agrarian revolution, the right of self-determination of the Negro population would be only a Utopia, or at best would remain only on paper without changing in any way the actual enslavement.

(2) *Establishment of the State Unity of the Black Belt.* At the present time this Negro zone—precisely for the purpose of facilitating national oppression—is artificially split up and divided into a number of various states which include distant localities having a majority of white population. If the right of self-determination of the Negroes is to be put into force, it is necessary wherever possible to bring together into one governmental unit all districts of the South where the majority of the settled population consists of Negroes. Within the limits of this state there will of course remain a fairly significant white minority which must submit to the right of self-determination of the Negro majority. There is no other possible way of carrying out in a democratic manner the right of self-determination of the Negroes. Every plan regarding the establishment of the Negro State with an exclusively Negro population in America (and, of course, still more exporting it to Africa) is nothing but an unreal and reactionary caricature of the fulfillment of the right of self-determination of the Negroes and every at-

tempt to isolate and transport the Negroes would have the most damaging effect upon their interests; above all, it would violate the right of the Negro farmers in the Black Belt not only to their present residences and their land but also to the land owned by the white landlords and cultivated by Negro labour.

(3) *Right of Self-Determination.* This means complete and unlimited right of the Negro majority to exercise governmental authority in the entire territory of the Black Belt, as well as to decide upon the relations between their territory and other nations, particularly the United States. It would not be right of self-determination in our sense of the word if the Negroes in the Black Belt had the right of determination only in cases which concerned *exclusively* the Negroes and did not affect the whites, because the most important cases arising here are bound to affect the Negroes as well as the whites. First of all, true right to self-determination means that the Negro majority and not the white minority in the entire territory of the administratively united Black Belt exercises the right of administrating governmental, legislative and judicial authority. At the present time all this power here is concentrated in the hands of the white bourgeoisie and landlords. It is they who appoint all officials, it is they who dispose of public property, it is they who determine the taxes, it is they who govern and make the laws. Therefore, *the overthrow of this class rule* in the Black Belt is unconditionally necessary in the struggle for the Negroes' right to self-determination. This, however, means at the same time the overthrow of the yoke of American imperialism in the Black Belt on which the forces of the local white bourgeoisie depend. Only in this way, only if the Negro population of the Black Belt wins its freedom from American imperialism even to the point of deciding itself the relations between its country and other governments, especially the United States, will it win real and complete self-determination. One should demand from the beginning that no armed forces of American imperialism should remain on the territory of the Black Belt.

7. As stated in the letter of the Polit. Secretariat of the E.C.C.I. of March 16th, 1930, the Communists must *"unreservedly* carry on a struggle" for the self-determination of the Negro population in the Black Belt in accordance with what has been set forth above. It is incorrect and harmful to interpret the Communist standpoint to mean that the Communists stand for the right of self-determination of the Negroes only up to a certain point, but not beyond this, for example, to the right of separation. It is also incorrect to say that the Communists are so far only to carry on propaganda or agitation for the right of self-determination, but not to develop any activity to bring this about. No, it is of the utmost importance for the Communist Party to reject any such limitation of its struggle for this slogan. Even if the situation does not yet warrant the raising of the question of uprising, one should not limit

oneself at present to propaganda for the demand: "Right to self-determination," but should organize mass actions, such as demonstrations, strikes, tax-boycott-movements, etc.

Moreover, the Party cannot make its stand for this slogan dependent upon any conditions, even the condition that the proletariat has the hegemony in the national revolutionary Negro movement or that the majority of the Negroes in the Black Belt adopts the Soviet form (as Pepper demanded), etc.. It goes without saying that the Communists in the Black Belt will and must try to win over all working elements of the Negroes, that is, the majority of the population, to their side and to convince them not only that they must win the right of self-determination, but also that they must make use of this right in accordance with the Communist programme. But this cannot be made a *condition* for the stand of the Communists in favor of the right of self-determination of the Negro population; if, or so long as the majority of this population wishes to handle the situation in the Black Belt in a different manner from that which we Communists would like, its complete right to self-determination must be recognized. This right we must defend as a free democratic right.

8. In general, the C.P. of the United States has kept to this correct line recently in its struggle for the right of self-determination of the Negroes even though this line—in some cases—has been unclearly or erroneously expressed. In particular some misunderstanding has arisen from the failure to make a clear distinction between the demand for "right of self-determination" and the demand for governmental separation, simply treating these two demands in the same way. However, these two demands are not identical. Complete right to self-determination includes also the right to governmental separation, but does not necessarily imply that the Negro population should *make use of this* right under all circumstances, that is, that it must actually separate or attempt to separate the Black Belt from the existing governmental federation with the United States. If it desires to separate it must be free to do so; but if it prefers to remain federated with the United States it must also be free to do that. This is the correct meaning of the idea of self-determination and it must be recognized quite independently of whether the United States are still a capitalist state or if a proletarian dictatorship has already been established there.

It is, however, another matter if it is not a case of the *right* of the oppressed nation concerned to separate or to maintain governmental contact, but if the question is treated on its merits; whether it is to work for state separation, whether it is to struggle *for this* or not. This is another question, on which the stand of the Communists must vary according to the concrete conditions. If the proletariat has come into power in the United States, the

Communist Negroes will not come out for but *against* separation of the Negro Republic federation with the United States. But the *right* of the Negroes to governmental separation will be *unconditionally realized* by the Communist Party, it will unconditionally give the Negro population of the Black Belt freedom of choice even on this question. Only when the proletariat has come into power in the United States the Communists will carry on propaganda among the working masses of the Negro population against separation, in order to convince them that it is much better and in the interest of the Negro nation for the Black Belt to be a free republic, where the Negro majority has complete right of self-determination but remains governmentally federated with the great proletarian republic of the United States. The bourgeois counterrevolutionists on the other hand will then be interested in boosting the separation tendencies in the ranks of the various nationalities in order to utilize separatist nationalism as a barrier for the bourgeois counter-revolution against the consolidation of the proletarian dictatorship.

But the question at the present time is not this. As long as capitalism rules in the United States the Communists cannot come out against governmental separation of the Negro zone from the United States. They recognize that this separation from the imperialist United States would be preferable from the standpoint of the national interests of the Negro population, to their present oppressed state, and therefore, the Communists are ready at any time to offer all their support if only the working masses of the Negro population are ready to take up the struggle for governmental independence of the Black Belt. At the present time, however, the situation in the national struggle in the South is not such as to win mass support of the working Negroes for this separatist struggle; and it is not the task of the Communists to call upon them to separate without taking into consideration the existing situation and the desires of the Negro masses.

The situation in the Negro question of the United States, however, may undergo a radical change. It is even probable that the separatist efforts to obtain complete State independence of the Black Belt will gain ground among the Negro masses of the South in the near future. This is connected with the prospective sharpening of the national conflicts in the South, with the advance of the national revolutionary Negro movement and with the exceptionally brutal fascists aggressiveness of the white exploiters of the South, as well as with the support of this aggressiveness by the central government authority of the United States. In this sharpening of the situation in the South, Negro separatism will presumably increase, and the question of the independence of the Black Belt will become the question of the day. Then the Communist Party must also face this question and, if the circumstances seem favorable, must stand up with all strength and courage for the struggle to win independence and for the establishment of a Negro republic in the Black Belt.

9. The general relation of Communists to separatist tendencies among the Negroes, described above, cannot mean that Communists associate themselves at present, or generally speaking, during capitalism, indiscriminately and without criticism with all the separatist currents of the various bourgeois or petty-bourgeois Negro groups. For there is not only a national revolutionary, but also a reactionary Negro separatism, for instance, that represented by Garvey; his Utopia of an isolated Negro State (regardless if in Africa or America, if it is supposed to consist of Negroes only) pursues the only political aim of diverting the Negro masses from the real liberation struggle against American imperialism.

It would be a mistake to imagine that the right of self-determination slogan is a truly revolutionary slogan only in connection with the demand for complete separation. The question of power is decided not only through the demand of separation, but just as much through the demand of the right to decide the separation question and self-determination in general. A direct question of power is also the demand of confiscation of the land of the white exploiters in the South, as well as the demand of the Negroes that the entire Black Belt be amalgamated into a State unit.

Hereby, every single fundamental demand of the liberation struggle of the Negroes in the Black Belt is such that—if once thoroughly understood by the Negro masses and adopted as their slogan—it will lead them into the struggle for the overthrow of the power of the ruling bourgeoisie, which is impossible without such revolutionary struggle. One cannot deny that it is just possible for the Negro population of the Black Belt to win the right to self-determination already during capitalism; but it is perfectly clear and indubitable that this is possible only through successful revolutionary struggle for power against the American bourgeoisie, through wresting the Negroes' right to self-determination from the American imperialism. Thus, the slogan of right to self-determination is a real slogan of national rebellion which, to be considered as such, need not be supplemented by proclaiming struggle for the complete separation of the Negro zone, at least not at present. But it must be made perfectly clear to the Negro masses that the slogan "right to self-determination" includes the demand of full freedom for them to decide even the question of complete separation. "We demand freedom of separation, real right to self-determination"—wrote Lenin: "certainly not in order to 'recommend' separation, but on the contrary, in order to facilitate and accelerate the democratic rapprochement and unification of nations." For the same purpose, Lenin's Party, the C.P. of the Soviet Union, bestowed after its seizure of power on all the peoples hitherto oppressed by Russian Tsarism the full right to self-determination, including the right of complete separation, and achieved thereby its enormous successes with regard to the democratic rapprochement and voluntary unification of nations.

10. The slogan for the self-determination right and the other fundamental slogans of the Negro question in the Black Belt does not exclude but rather pre-supposes an energetic development of the struggle for concrete partial demands linked up with the daily needs and afflictions of wide masses of working Negroes. In order to avoid, in this connection, the danger of opportunist back-slidings, Communists must above all remember this:

(a) The direct aims and partial demands around which a partial struggle develops are to be linked up in the course of the struggle with the revolutionary fundamental slogans brought up by the question of power, in a popular manner corresponding to the mood of the masses. (Confiscation of the big land-holdings, establishment of governmental unity of the Black Belt, right of self-determination of the Negro population in the Black Belt.) Bourgeois-socialist tendencies to oppose such a revolutionary widening and deepening of the fighting demands must be fought.

(b) One should not venture to draw up a complete programme of some kind or a system of "positive" partial demands. Such programmes on the part of petty-bourgeois politicians should be exposed as attempts to divert the masses from the necessary hard struggles by fostering reformist and democratic illusions among them. Every positive partial demand which might crop up is to be considered from the viewpoint of whether it is in keeping with our revolutionary fundamental slogans, or whether it is of a reformist or reactionary tendency. Every kind of national oppression which arouses the indignation of the Negro masses can be used as a suitable point of departure for the development of partial struggles, during which the abolition of such oppression, as well as their prevention through revolutionary struggle against the ruling exploiting dictatorship must be demanded.

(c) Everything should be done to bring wide masses of Negroes into these partial struggles—this is important—and not to carry the various partial demands to such an ultra-radical point, that the mass of working Negroes are no longer able to recognize them as *their own*. Without a real mobilisation of the mass-movements—in spite of the sabotage of the bourgeois reformist Negro politicians—even the best Communist partial demands get hung up. On the other hand, even some relatively insignificant acts of the Ku-Klux-Klan bandits in the Black Belt can become the occasion of important political movements, provided the Communists are able to organise the resistance of the indignant Negro masses. In such cases, mass movements of this kind can easily develop into real rebellion. This rests on the fact that—as Lenin said—"Every act of national oppression calls forth resistance on the part of the masses of the population, and the tendency of every act of resistance on the part of oppressed peoples is the national uprising."

d) Communists must fight in the *forefront* of the national-liberation movement and must do their utmost for the progress of this mass movement and its revolutionisation. Negro Communists must *clearly dissociate* themselves from all bourgeois currents in the Negro movement, must indefatigably oppose the spread of the influence of the bourgeois groups on the working Negroes, and in dealing with them must apply the Communist tactic laid down by the Sixth C.I. Congress with regard to the colonial question, in order to guarantee the *hegemony of the Negro proletariat* in the national liberation movement of the Negro population, and to co-ordinate wide masses of the Negro peasantry in a steady fighting alliance with the proletariat.

e) One must work with the utmost energy for the establishment and consolidation of *Communist Party organisations and* revolutionary *trade unions* in the South. Furthermore, immediate measures must be taken for the organisation of proletarian and peasant *self-defense* of whites and blacks against the Ku-Klux-Klan; for this purpose, the C.P. is to give further instructions.

11. It is particularly incumbent on Negro Communists to criticize consistently the half-heartedness and hesitations of the petty-bourgeois national-revolutionary Negro leaders in the liberation struggle of the Black Belt, exposing them before the masses. All national reformist currents as, for instance, Garveyism, which are an obstacle to the revolutionisation of the Negro masses, must be fought systematically and with the utmost energy. Simultaneously, Negro Communists must carry on among the Negro masses an energetic struggle against nationalist moods directed indiscriminately against all whites, workers as well as capitalists, Communists, as well as imperialists. Their constant call to the Negro masses must be: *revolutionary struggle against the ruling white bourgeoisie, through a fighting alliance with the revolutionary white proletariat!* Negro Communists must indefatigably explain to the mass of the Negro population that even if many white workers in America are still infected with Negrophobia, the American proletariat, as a class, which owing to its struggle against the American bourgeoisie represents the only truly revolutionary class, will be the only real mainstay of Negro liberation. In as far as successes in the national-revolutionary struggle of the Negro population of the South for its right to self-determination are already possible under capitalism, they can be achieved only if this struggle is effectively supported by proletarian mass actions on a large scale in the other parts of the United States. But it is also clear that "only a victorious proletarian revolution will *finally* decide the agrarian question and the national question in the South of the United States, in the

interest of the predominating mass of the Negro population of the country."
(Colonial Theses of the Sixth World Congress.)

12. The struggle regarding the Negro question in the North must be
linked up with the liberation struggle in the South, in order to endow the
Negro movement throughout the United States with the necessary effective
strength. After all, in the North as well as in the South, it is a question of the
real emancipation of the American Negroes which has in fact never taken
place before. The Communist Party of the United States must bring into play
its entire revolutionary energy in order to mobilize the widest possible
masses of the white and black proletariat of the United States, not by words,
but by deeds, for real effective support of the struggle for the liberation of
the Negroes. Enslavement of the Negroes is one of the most important foun-
dations of the imperialist dictatorship of U.S.A. capitalism. The more
American imperialism fastens its yoke on the millions strong Negro masses,
the more must the Communist Party develop the mass struggle for Negro
emancipation, and the better use it must make of all conflicts which arise out
of national differences, as an incentive for revolutionary mass actions against
the bourgeoisie. This is as much in the direct interest of the proletarian revolution in America. Whether the rebellion of the Negroes is to be the outcome
of a general revolutionary situation in the United States, whether it is to
originate in the whirlpool of decisive fights for power by the working-class,
for proletarian dictatorship, or whether on the contrary, the Negro rebellion
will be the prelude of gigantic struggles for power by the American proletariat, cannot be foretold now. But in either contingency, it is essential for the
Communist Party *to make an energetic beginning already now* with the organisation of *joint mass struggles* of white and black workers against Negro
oppression. This alone will enable us to get rid of the bourgeois white chauvinism which is polluting the ranks of the white workers of America, to
overcome the distrust of the Negro masses caused by the inhuman barbarous
Negro slave traffic still carried on by the American bourgeoisie—in as far as
it is directed even against all white workers—and to win over to our side
these millions of Negroes as active fellow fighters in the struggle for the
overthrow of bourgeois power throughout America.

SELECTED BIBLIOGRAPHY

Anderson, Carol. "Bleached Souls and Red Negroes: the NAACP and Black Communists in the Early Cold War, 1948-1952." In *The Achievement of American Liberalism: The New Deal and Its Legacies*, edited by William Henry Chafe. New York: Columbia University Press, 2003.

Allen, James S. *Negro Liberation*. New York: International Publishers, 1938.

Baldwin, Kate A. *Beyond the Color Line and the Iron Curtain: Reading Encounters Between Black and Red,1922-1963*. Durham, N.C.: Duke University Press, 2002.

Berland, Oscar. "The Communist Perspective on the 'Negro Question' in America, 1919-1931." *Science & Society* 63 and 64, no. 4/2 (Winter-Summer 1999-2000).

———. "Nasanov and the Comintern's American Negro Program." *Science & Society* 65, no. 2 (2001).

Blakely, Allison. *Russia and the Negro: Blacks in Russian History and Thought*. Washington, DC: Howard University Press, 1986.

Bornet, Vaughn D. "Historical Scholarship, Communism, and the Negro." *The Journal of Negro History* 37 (July 1952).

Burghardt, W. and Joyce Moore Turner, eds., *Richard B. Moore, Caribbean Militant In Harlem: Collected Writings, 1920-1972*. Bloomington: University of Indiana Press, 1989.

Campbell, Susan. "'Black Bolsheviks' and Recognition of African-America's Right to Self-Determination by the Communist Party USA." *Science & Society* 58, no. 4 (1994/95).

Carter, Dan T. *Scottsboro: A Tragedy of the American South*. Baton Rouge: Louisiana State University Press, 1979.

Davis, Benjamin J. *Communist Councilman from Harlem: Autobiographical Notes Written in a Federal Penitentiary*. New York: International Publishers, 1969.

Edwards, Brent Hayes. "Dossier on Black Radicalism: Introduction: The Autonomy of Black Radicalism." *Social Text* 19 (2001).

Eversole, Theodore W. "Benjamin J. Davis, Jr. (1903-1964): From Republican Atlanta Lawyer to Harlem Communist Councilman." *Journal of the Afro-American Historical and Genealogical Society* 8 (1987).

Foner, Philip Sheldon. *American Socialism and Black Americans from the Age of Jackson to World War II*. Westport, CT: Greenwood Press, 1977.

———, and James S. Allen, eds. *American Communism and Black Americans: A Documentary History, 1919-1929*. Philadelphia: Temple University Press, 1987.

———, and Herbert Shapiro, eds. *American Communism and Black Americans: A Documentary History, 1930-1934*. Philadelphia: Temple University Press, 1991.

Ford, James W. *The Negro and the Democratic Front*. New York: International Publishers, 1938.

Garder, John L. "African Americans in the Soviet Union in the 1920s and 1930s: The Development of Transcontinental Protest." *Western Journal of Black Studies* 23 (1999).

Goldfield, Michael. "The Decline of the Communist Party and the Black Question in the U.S.: Harry Haywood's Black Bolshevik." *Review of Radical Political Economics* 12 (1980).

Goodman, James E. *Stories of Scottsboro*. New York: Pantheon Books, 1994.

Grigsby, Daryl Russell. *For the People: Black Socialists in the United States, Africa, and the Caribbean*. San Diego: Asante Publications, 1987.

Haywood, Harry. *The Road to Negro Liberation: The Tasks of the Communist Party In Winning Working Class Leadership of the Negro Liberation Struggles, and the Fight Against Reactionary Nationalist-Reformist Movements Among the Negro People*. New York: Workers Library, 1934.

————. *Black Bolshevik: Autobiography of an Afro-American Communist*. Chicago: Liberator Press, 1978.

Hill, Robert A. "Racial and Radical: Cyril V. Briggs, *The Crusader* Magazine, and the African Blood Brotherhood, 1918-1922." New York: Garland Publishing, 1987.

Horne, Gerald. *Black Liberation/Red Scare: Ben Davis and the Communist Party*. Newark, DE: University of Delaware Press, 1993.

————. *Studies in Black: Progressive Views and Reviews of the African-American Experience*. Dubuque, IA: Kendall/Hunt, 1992.

————. "The Red and the Black: The Communist Party and African-Americans in Historical Perspective." In *New Studies in the Politics and Culture of U.S. Communism*, edited by Michael E. Brown, Randy Martin, Frank Rosengarten, and George Snedeker. New York: Monthly Review Press, 1993.

————. *Powell v. Alabama: The Scottsboro Boys and American Justice*. New York: Franklin Watts, 1977.

Huiswood, Otto. "Speech to the Third International," *International Press Correspondence* 3, 5 January 1923, 14-16.

Hutchinson, Earl Ofari. *Blacks and Reds: Race and Class in Conflict, 1919-1990*. East Lansing: Michigan State University Press, 1995.

Jackson, James. *Revolutionary Tracings*. New York: International Publishers, 1974.

James, Winston. *Holding Aloft the Banner of Ethiopia: Caribbean Radicalism in Early Twentieth-Century America*. London, New York: Verso, 1998.

Johanningsmeier, Edward. "Communists and Black Freedom Movements in South Africa and the US: 1919-1950." *Journal of Southern African Studies* 30 (March 2004).

Kanet, Roger. "The Comintern and the 'Negro Question': Communist Policy in the United States and Africa, 1921-1941." *Survey [U.K.]* 19 (Autumn 1973).

Kelley, Robin D. G. *Hammer and Hoe: Alabama Communists during the Great Depression*. Chapel Hill: University of North Carolina Press, 1984.

————. *Race Rebels: Culture, Politics, and the Black Working Class*. New York and Toronto: Free Press and Maxwell Macmillan, 1994.

————. "But a Local Phase of World Problem: Black History's Global Vision, 1883-1950." *Journal of American History* 86 (December 1999).

————. "'Comrades, Praise Gawd for Lenin and Them!': Ideology and Culture Among Black Communists in Alabama, 1930-1935," *Science and Society* 52/1 (Spring 1988).

Klehr, Harvey, and William Tompson. "Self-Determination in the Black Belt: Origins of a Communist Policy." *Labor History* 30 (Summer 1989): 354-66.

Kosa, John, and Clyde Z. Nunn. "Race, Deprivation and Attitude Toward Communism." *Phylon* 25 (1964).

Klore, Joe. "Harlem's Communist Councilman, Ben Davis Jr." *Political Affairs* 81 (2002).

McClellan, Woodford. "Africans and Black Americans in the Comintern Schools, 1925 -1934." *International Journal of African Historical Studies* 2 (1993): 371-90.

Marable, Manning. "Why Black Americans Are not Socialists." In *Socialist Per-*

spectives, ed. by Phyllis Jacobson and Julius Jacobson, assisted by Petr Abovin-Egides. Princeton, NJ: Karz-Cohl Pub., 1983.

Markowitz, Norman. "Benjamin Davis, Jr.: Centennial, 1903-2003." *Political Affairs* 82 (February 2003).

Martin, Charles H. "The International Labor Defense and Black Americans." *Labor History* 26 (Spring 1985).

Maxwell, William. *New Negro, Old Left: African American Writing and Communism Between the Wars*. New York: Columbia University Press, 1999.

Miller, James A., Susan D. Pennybacker, and Eve Rosenhaft. "Mother Ada Wright and the International Campaign to Free the Scottsboro Boys." *American Historical Review* 106 (April 2001).

Miller, Sally M. *Race, Ethnicity, and Gender in Early Twentieth-Century American Socialism*. Garland Reference Library of Social Science, vol. 880. New York and London: Garland Publishing, 1996.

Murray, Hugh T., Jr. "The NAACP Versus the Communist Party: The Scottsboro Rape Cases, 1931-1932." *Phylon* 28 (1967).

———. "Aspects of the Scottsboro Campaign." *Science and Society* 35 (Summer 1971).

———. "Changing America and the Changing Image of Scottsboro." *Phylon*, March 1977.

Naison, Mark. "Marxism and Black Radicalism in America: Notes on a Long (and Continuing) Journey." *Radical America* 5 (May-June 1971).

———. "Communism and Black Nationalism in the Depression: The Case of Harlem." *Journal of Ethnic Studies* 2 (Summer 1974).

———. "The Communist Party in Harlem: 1928-1936." Ph.D. diss. Columbia University, 1976.

———. "The Communist Party in Harlem in the Early Depression Years: A Case Study in the Reinterpretation of American Communism." *Radical History Review*, no. 3 (Fall 1976).

———. "Harlem Communists and the Politics of Black Protest." *Marxist Perspectives* 1, no. 3 (Fall 1978).

———. "Historical Notes on Blacks and American Communism: The Harlem Experience." *Science and Society* 42, no. 3 (Fall 1978).

———. *Communists in Harlem during the Depression*. Urbana: University of Illinois Press, 1983.

Nolan, William Anthony. *Communism Versus the Negro*. Chicago: H. Regnery Co., 1951.

Norris, Clarence. *The Last of the Scottsboro Boys*. New York, Putnam, 1979.

Patterson, Haywood with Earl Conrad, *Scottsboro Boy* (New York: Collier Books, 1969).

Patterson, William L. *The Man Who Cried Genocide: An Autobiography*. New York: International Publishers, 1971.

Peterson, Dale. *Up From Bondage: The Literatures of Russian and African American Soul*. Durham, N.C.: Duke University, 2000.

Record, Wilson. "American Racial Ideologies and Organizations in Transition." *Phylon* 26 (Winter 1965).

———. *The Negro and the Communist Party*. Chapel Hill: University of North Carolina Press, 1951.

———. "The Development of the Communist Position on the Negro Question in the

United States." *Phylon* 19 (Fall 1958).

————. *Race and Radicalism: The NAACP and the Communist Party in Conflict.* Ithaca, NY: Cornell University Press, 1964.

Robinson, Cedric. *Black Marxism: The Making of the Black Radical Tradition.* Chapel Hill: University of North Carolina Press, 2000.

Rywkin, Michael. "Black Americans: A Race or Nationality? Some Communist Viewpoints." *Canadian Review of Studies in Nationalism* 3, no. 1 (1975).

Solomon, Mark. "Red and Black: Negroes and Communism, 1929-1932." Ph.D. diss. Harvard University, 1972.

————. *Red and Black: Communism and Afro-Americans, 1929-1935.* New York: Garland Pub., 1988.

————. *The Cry Was Unity: Communists and African Americans, 1917-36.* Jackson: University Press of Mississippi, 1998.

Spark, Clare. "Race, Caste, or Class? The Bunche-Myrdal Dispute Over An American Dilemma." *International Journal of Politics, Culture, and Society* 14, no. 3 (Spring 2001).

Sullivan, William C. "Communism and the American Negro." *Religion in Life* 37, no. 4 (1968).

Thomas, Tony. "Black Nationalism and Confused Marxists." *Black Scholar* 4 (1972).

Van West, Carroll. "Perpetuating the Myth of America: Scottsboro and Its Interpreters." *South Atlantic Quarterly* 80 (1981).

Van Zanter, John W. "Communist Theory and the American Negro Question." *Review of Politics* 29, no. 4 (1967).

Wald, Alan. "New Black Radical Scholarship." *Against the Current*, no. 108 (January- February 2004).

————. "The U.S. Left and Anti-Racism." In *Black Liberation and the American Dream: The Struggle for Racial and Economic Justice: Analysis, Strategy, Readings*, edited by Paul Le Blanc. Revolutionary Studies. Amherst, N.Y.: Humanity Books, 2003.

Wexley, John. "They Shall Not Die." In *Proletarian Literature in the United States: An Anthology*, edited by Granville Hicks and Joseph Freeman. New York: International Publishers, 1935.

Williams, Henry. *Black Response to the American Left: 1917-1929.* Princeton, N.J.: Princeton University, 1973.

Williams, Lynn Barstis. "Images of Scottsboro." *Southern Cultures* 6, no. 1 (2000).

Wynn, Daniel Webster. *The NAACP Versus Negro Revolutionary Protest: A Comparative Study of the Effectiveness of Each Movement.* New York: Exposition Press, 1955.

ABOUT THE EDITOR

Walter T. Howard holds a M.A. in history from the University of West Florida and a Ph.D. in American history from Florida State University. He is currently Professor of History at Bloomsburg University, a small state university in northeastern Pennsylvania. He has written numerous books and journal articles about African American history, U.S. labor history and American Communism.

INDEX

www.ingramcontent.com/pod-product-compliance
Lightning Source LLC
Chambersburg PA
CBHW050522280326
41932CB00014B/2422